C000140107

E⋯⋯⋯⋯⋯⋯s

First Edition

ISBN: 0 85052 777 5

Price £4.95

There are special rates for purchases of more than 10 books

Pen & Sword Books Ltd
47 Church Street
Barnsley S70 2AS

Telephone: 01226 734222   Fax: 01226 734438

Email: enquiries@pen-and-sword.co.uk
Website:www.pen-and-sword.co.uk

The Information in this publication has been gathered from unclassified sources.

Front Cover: Photograph courtesy of the City of London Police.

Rear Cover: Photograph courtesy of Dorset Police.
Helicopter; MD902 Explorer

Police Service Statement of Common Purpose and Values

"The purpose of the police service is to uphold the law fairly; to prevent crime; to pursue and bring to justice those who break the law; to keep the Queen's Peace; to protect, help and reassure the community; and to be seen to do all this with integrity, common sense and sound judgement.

We must be compassionate, courteous and patient, acting without fear or favour or prejudice to the rights of others. We need to be professional, calm and restrained in the face of violence and apply only that force which is necessary to accomplish our lawful duty.

We must strive to reduce the fears of the public and, so far as we can, to reflect their priorities in the action we take. We must respond to well founded criticism with a willingness to change."

(Source: Association of Chief Police Officers)

Preface to First Edition

Writing this book has been a mammoth, but worthwhile, undertaking. We trust that the details for each Force are of real value to the reader. However, as this is the first book of this kind on the UK police we would appreciate being informed of additional information which readers wish to see in future editions. We have tried to produce the figures in a meaningful way, such as the cost per resident per day of their police service and the number of selected crimes.

Statistics are complex and are merely indicators for the guidance of the wise. The fact that a Force has a low crime rate does not necessarily mean that it is effective; it could be that people lack confidence in their police and therefore do not bother to report offences. Similarly, a high crime rate may not mean that a Force is ineffective; it could indicate that people feel confident that reporting offences will lead to arrests being made. Although it is perceived wisdom that Forces want crime levels to reduce there are occasions when they expect, and hope for a rise. The rise in the reported level of hate crimes, i.e., racially motivated, domestic and homophobic, suggest that the climate in society makes people feel more confident in reporting such crimes. Obviously at some stage the police believe that the reported levels of hate crimes will plateau and reduce as their efforts to tackle these offences have an impact. The cost of policing in London appear to be higher than county areas, however the Metropolitan Police Service do carry out work which have national implications. Statistics are a valuable indicator of performance, but they are not the whole story.

The impact of the Lawrence Inquiry (and the Macpherson Report which followed) coupled with the implementation of Human Rights legislation will have a significant impact on policing. Areas of concern, such as ethnic minority representation in the police, racial incidents and stop and search figures, feature prominently in this book.

Comments, observations or constructive criticisms are welcomed. Letters addressed to 'The Editor - UK Police Guide' care of Pen & Sword Books Ltd, 47 Church Street, Barnsley, S70 2AS or e-mails to: glyn.collins@rya-online.net will receive prompt attention.

This guide has been produced wholly independently and the information has been gleaned from annual reports, the internet and other open sources. Any opinions expressed are not to be construed as representing the view of the police, or any section of the police.

Our thanks go to the good people at Pen & Sword Books for having the confidence to add this book to their pocket guide series and for their help and encouragement. We would like to express our appreciation to the many people in Forces across the country who assisted in supplying us with information so generously, without their help this book could not have been written. The credit for the information in this book is theirs; we regret that any errors, inaccuracies or omissions are ours.

Finally, thanks goes to all our police colleagues; ordinary people doing an extraordinary job.

M. J. McBride / G. D. Collins

FOREWORD

Although we, the police, can be proud of our achievements there remain areas for improved performance. It is only through transparency and a willingness to enter into a constructive dialogue with our communities that positive change can occur.

Our policing model is still held in high regard throughout the world. The image of the 'British Bobby' has almost become a national icon. In spite of all the interest in the subject, the reality of police work remains a mystery for most people who have never been a police officer, donned a uniform and pounded a beat. This does not stop people criticising their local police and in our democracy the public should feel free to air their views. The aim of this book is to make policing more open and to better inform the reader. In one pocket sized book you have really useful information about one of this country's best assets, its Police Service.

The performance figures in this guide only give one insight into the reality of policing. Much police activity goes unrecorded, but is no less important to the residents of the communities we serve and depend upon for their continued support.

The information included, and omitted, from this guide reflects policing itself. There is always more to be done than can be done. Although we constantly strive to serve the public we are acutely aware that there will never be enough resources for every expectation to be met. This calls for difficult decisions to be made.

It is hoped that through our Annual Reports, websites and this guide an informed debate can take place to make significant progress for the future of policing.

Mr Nigel Burgess, Q.P.M.
Chief Constable
Cheshire Constabulary

CONTENTS

The Police Service

Any civilisation or country, whether a democracy or otherwise, will require laws and rules. Each nation has a force of men and women, mostly professional, sometimes voluntary, whose job it is to uphold and enforce the laws of that land.

The Police service of the United Kingdom is regarded globally as one of the finest in the world.

The service is based on the office of constables, who is defined as a person 'locally appointed'. Police Officers are usually sworn into office by local magistrates.

The functions of a constable are fourfold.

The preservation of life and property
The preservation of order
The prevention and detection of crime
The prosecution of offenders against the peace

As can be seen from the Association of Chief Police Officers statement of common purpose and values. It is the fundamental aim of the Police in this country to deliver its duties fairly and with the consent of the public that it serves.

On attestation at the start of an officer's career, the new constable will swear an oath as set out by Schedule 2 of the Police Act 1964;

"I do solemnly and sincerely declare and affirm that I will well and truly serve Our Sovereign Lady The Queen in the office of constables without favour or affection, malice or ill will; and that I will to the best of my power cause the peace to be kept and preserved; and prevent all offences against the persons and properties of Her Majesty's subjects; and that, while I continue to hold that said office, I will to the best of my skill and knowledge discharge all the duties thereof faithfully according to law."

It has been said that Britain gets the Police Service that it deserves. The people of the country elect the government, the electorate making its choice mostly on an election manifesto, or from previous experience. The people will know the government's stance on policing and law and order issues. Laws are made and repealed by parliament. The Police, who operate within the law and codes of conduct and practice, uphold those laws.

Thus, in all respects, from appointment, through to operation and remit, the Police Forces of the United Kingdom are part of, and are there to serve, the people of the country.

CHAPTER 1. THE DEVELOPMENT OF POLICING

The model of policing we see in Britain today is a product of many changes that have occurred over time. To understand why the police service is structured, equipped and operated as it is, requires an appreciation of the evolutionary events that have shaped it through its history. Over the past centuries the police service has evolved into a professional body serving the needs of the community, by ensuring public safety and preventing and detecting crime. In short, to make the country a safe and habitable place in which to live. This chapter outlines the milestone events that have shaped the service.

1066 - The Middle Ages
The Normans were one of the earliest influences. Modern Coroners' Courts can trace their origin back to Norman times, where an inquisition was held to establish the cause of death of a found body. The title 'Constable' is derived from the Norman phrase for 'keeper of horses'. However, during the Middle Ages, the concept of a separate police force was alien, as it was expected that every person had a duty to keep law and order.
Terms such as 'hue and cry' still persist today, harking back to the Anglo-Saxon era when it was everyone's duty to catch felons.

1285 - Statute of Winchester
The Statute of Winchester laid down the principles of common law, which still exist today, such as the right to make a 'citizen's arrest'. The statute also introduced watchmen, under the direction of a constable, to oversee their part of the town.

1361 - Justice of Peace Act
The present system of Magistrates (Justices of the Peace - J.P.s) to deal with local law and order dates back to the Justice of the Peace Act. These justices could issue warrants instructing constables to make arrests. This still exists today.

1663 - City of London
Paid night watchmen, nicknamed 'Charlies', were introduced into The City of London. The low pay only attracted elderly or disabled men and were therefore not an effective force.

1750 - Improvement Act
Industrialisation and a burgeoning population led to a rise in urban crime in many towns and cities. Improvement Commissioners established a night watch of paid constables to patrol the streets.

1750 - Bow Street Runners
Established by Henry Fielding, chief magistrate for Westminster in London, The Bow Street Runners were the first paid police officers.

1800 - Thames River Police
To combat crime, predominantly the widespread theft of cargoes and boats, on London's River Thames, the Thames River Police were formed into a force paid directly by the Home Office. This force still exists today as an integral part of the Metropolitan Police.

1805 - Bow Street Horse Patrol
Forty-four former cavalrymen were used to patrol the highways of London. These mounted patrols were armed with pistols, swords and truncheons.

1819 - Peterloo Massacre
The use of local cavalry militia to disperse a large crowd in St Peter's Fields, Manchester (the Peterloo Massacre) who had gathered to hear Orator Hunt led to the deaths of 11 innocent people and the growing realisation that a non-military option for the control of such incidents, was long overdue.

1822 - Irish Constabulary
The first organised policing in Ireland came with the formation of the Irish Constabulary.

1829 - Metropolitan Police
In the post-Napoleonic era Sir Robert Peel, the Home Secretary, laid down the precepts for the first modern police force - the Metropolitan Police in London. Some three thousand officers were recruited, and by 1836, they incorporated the Bow Street Runners, the Thames River Police and the Horse Patrol. The City of London, the 'square mile', was and still is, policed by a separate force (City of London Police - see 1838).

1831 - Special Constabulary
Local magistrates appointed the first Special Constables, unpaid local volunteers.

1833 - Coldbath Fields Riots, London
The recently formed Metropolitan police, known as 'Peelers' or 'Bobbies', initially received a hostile reception from the public. During the Coldbath Fields Riots PC Robert Culley was slain. The officer's killers were acquitted on the grounds of 'justifiable homicide' and a cup was struck for each member of the jury - the Culley Cup. Despite this setback police Forces were created rapidly in urban areas, counties and boroughs.

1835 - Municipal Corporations Act
Each new corporation was required to establish a police force and within twenty years there were more than two hundred forces in England and Wales.

1838 - City of London
The City of London Police was founded.

1842 - First Detectives
The fledgling CID, officers whose task was solely to detect crime, was established in London with only two inspectors and six sergeants.

1883 - Special Branch
To combat the spate of bombings from Irish revolutionaries the Special Branch was formed.

1910 - New Technology
The murderer Dr. Crippen was arrested after a transatlantic voyage. A radio message had

been sent to the ship's captain. This was the first recorded incidence of a suspect being arrested with the help of radio. The police have been at the forefront of new technology to assist in the fight against crime.

1913 - Police Union
The National Union of Police and Prison Officers was created to improve the working conditions and pay of its members. Dissatisfaction with pay and conditions led to the police strike in 1919. The Home Office later recognised the newly formed Police Federation as a staff association for officers from Constable to Chief Inspector. The police are prohibited from striking and a code of conduct was drawn up.

1914 - Women Police
During the First World War, women joined the police for the first time.

1922 - Irish Partition
The Partition of Ireland led to the creation of the Royal Ulster Constabulary in the north, and the Garda Siochan· in the new Republic.

1930 - Road Traffic Legislation
As a result of the tragic and rising death toll on the roads, the first Road Traffic Act was introduced to try to reduce it. The police / motorist interaction has been a key feature of policing ever since, as traffic density has increased.

1955 - 'Dixon'
The 'Dixon of Dock Green' television series started its two-decade run of programmes featuring PC (later Sergeant) George Dixon played by the actor Jack Warner. Dixon came to be fixed in the national psyche as the epitome of the firm, fair and friendly 'Bobby'.

1960 - Personal Radios
The 1960's saw the introduction of personal radios for patrol officers. This led to the demise of fixed foot beats and police telephone boxes as officers could now be deployed more effectively in their new blue and white patrol cars, nicknamed 'Pandas'. This pattern of patrol deployment largely still exists today.

1963 - Organised Crime
A robbery of a Royal Mail train, which led to the tragic death of the driver and netted the gang more than two million pounds, heralded the growth of organised crime. Police forces have had to co-operate and form regional and national squads to deal with organised criminal groups.

1964 - Police Act
Following a Royal Commission the Police Act established the tri-partite arrangement between the Home Secretary, Police Authorities and Chief Constables. The number of police forces in England and Wales was reduced by various amalgamations, the new force areas more accurately reflecting the geography of the communities they served.

1967 - Sex Equality

The Sex Discrimination Act gave equal pay for women officers. They worked alongside their male colleagues and their Women and Children departments were consigned to history.

1969 - The 'Troubles'

Widespread street disorder in Northern Ireland signalled the start of almost three decades of terrorism claiming the lives of thousands of civilians, soldiers and police officers. It forced a very different way of policing in the province.

1969 - Corruption

Police Corruption in the Metropolitan Police was raised in The Times. Various inquiries were conducted which included Operation Countryman in 1978 to investigate allegations of what the Chief Constable, Sir Robert Mark, called 'institutionalised corruption' in the Metropolitan Police.

The professional integrity of its members has always been a high priority for the police service and anti-corruption measures are in place.

1974 - Reorganisation

The local government reorganisations led to boundary changes and more amalgamations of smaller city and borough police forces with larger county and metropolitan ones.

1976 - Public Order Equipment

The need for protective equipment became crystal clear during the Notting Hill Carnival in London after the police resorted to using dustbin lids to protect themselves from missiles thrown at them. The following year, in 1977, police used newly acquired riot shields for the first time at a disturbance in South London between socialists and fascists.

1978 - Edmund Davies Report

Police pay was improved following a Committee of Enquiry into the Police. From this point onwards the police became an attractive career for graduates as it was rewarded financially as a profession rather than as a semi-skilled manual job.

1980 - Computerisation of Major Crime Inquiries

The Home Office Large and Major Enquiry System (HOLMES) was introduced to replace the traditional card index system used in major incident rooms to trace criminals. The investigation into Peter Sutcliffe, the Yorkshire Ripper, who murdered 13 women between 1975 and 1977, highlighted the inadequacies of a paper-based system. Although many clues to the identity of the Yorkshire Ripper were in the system, they were like needles in a haystack to find, and it took a simple stop-check by patrol officers to finally arrest Sutcliffe. Computer systems are now essential in the police response to crime. Other computer based emerging technologies are now embraced, such as automatic fingerprint recognition and DNA matching in the 1990's.

1981 - Inner-City Riots

Street disturbances in Brixton, South London, led to inner-city riots across the country. In the aftermath, the report by Lord Scarman recommended changes in community policing and race relations training.

1983 - Police Firearms Training.
In the hunt for a dangerous criminal, an innocent man, Stephen Waldorf, was mistaken for the criminal and shot by armed police in London. The resulting inquiry reduced the number of authorised firearms officers and improved their training. It also led to the ACPO 'Manual of Guidance on the Police Use of Firearms', which broadly governs the way firearms are deployed and officers are trained

1983 - Civilianisation
A Home Office circular (114/83) led to increased civilianisation of police posts. As a result the civilian support staff are now an essential and integral part of police Forces.

1984 - The Miners' Strike
A National Reporting Centre was created to co-ordinate the police officers from around the country needed to counter the flying pickets of striking miners. This was the first time that such an operation was run centrally raising the spectre of a, 'nationalised police force'. Since this time other national bodies have been established, such as National Criminal Intelligence Service, National Police Training and National Crime Squads.

1985 - Less Than Lethal Options
The horrific murder of PC Keith Blakelock during the Broadwater Farm Disorder in Tottenham, London, and ever-increasing violence towards officers, has, over the years since, renewed demands to arm the police. In response to such calls, but anxious to avoid arming, police officers have gradually acquired new equipment and training. The equipment consists of rigid-bar handcuffs, longer batons and, more recently, CS sprays. Body armour is now routinely worn for normal patrolling. Other options, such as pepper spray, and electric stun devices are being evaluated to fill the gap between the standard issue equipment and the use of firearms.

1987 - Armed Response Vehicles
In the aftermath of the killing spree in Hungerford, which involved the murder of 16 people by a gunman, Michael Ryan, police forces implemented reviews of their response to spontaneous firearms incidents. As a result, most forces deploy marked police cars, crewed by firearms officers, which are permanently equipped with firearms to respond rapidly to, and contain, firearms situations.

1993 - The Lawrence Inquiry
Following the murder of a black teenager, Stephen Lawrence, by white youths, a subsequent inquiry headed by Sir William Macpherson of Cluny, eventually led to a 70 point report in 1999, which criticised the police and other bodies, alleging 'institutionalised racism'.

1994 - Sheehy Report
Although the report on police structure, pay and conditions of service led by Sir Patrick Sheehy in the early 1990's was not fully implemented due to massive protest by police officers, some of its ideas were reflected in the Police and Magistrates' Courts Act. The Act gave chief officers greater freedom to manage their forces.

1998 - Partnership

Working with local authorities and other agencies to tackle local crime was the main thrust of the Crime and Disorder Act. This places a statutory obligation on these agencies to help fight crime.

1998 - National Crime Squad

It was formed from the former six Regional Crime Squads in response to a report from a Home Affairs Select Committee on The Threat of Organised Crime. The NCS has three areas, Northern, Eastern and Western. (See Chapter 2. Structure of the Service)

2000 - RUC Bravery Recognised

The Queen presented the George Cross, the highest civilian award for gallantry, to the Royal Ulster Constabulary.

2000 - Human Rights

The European Convention on Human Rights, which was modelled on English Law in the aftermath of the Second World War, was finally adopted by the UK. This may have an impact on surveillance operations, use of force and powers to stop and search.

2001 - Spedding

A commissioned report by Lord Spedding highlighted shortcomings in the gathering and sharing of intelligence between the various agencies. In the new era of intelligence led policing, The National Criminal Intelligence Service (NCIS) was given a statutory responsibility for the co-ordination of all intelligence.

2001 - Police Reform

Following the re-election of the Labour government, the new Home Secretary, David Blunkett, promised wide reform of the Police Service in Great Britain, with the introduction of a new Police Reform Bill. The reforms set out to challenge established practices and attitudes, setting up a Standards Unit, tackling sickness and increasing the numbers of uniformed officers on the streets.

2001 - War Against Terrorism

The terrorist atrocities in New York on 11th September, which claimed thousands of innocent lives, some British, resulted in the USA, Britain and many other countries in a new coalition, declaring a 'war against terrorism'.

The UK Police have since had to be ever more vigilant against further attacks on British soil; preventing backlashes against minorities; and in implementing new anti-terrorist legislation and policies.

2001 - Police Service of Northern Ireland

As one of many changes resulting from the Good Friday Agreement, the Patten report covering policing in the province of Northern Ireland recommended the re-naming of the Royal Ulster Constabulary. In November 2001 it became the Police Service of Northern Ireland.

CHAPTER 2. STRUCTURE OF THE SERVICE

The police service of the United Kingdom is generally classified into two broad parts. The first, and the most familiar to the public, are known as the Home Office forces. The other forces tend not to have a responsibility for a geographic area, but are usually concerned with railways, docks and other installations.

The Home Office Forces
The Home Office Forces are all the local police forces and everyone in the country lives in an area policed by one of them. They range from the big forces such as the Metropolitan Police service, the Greater Manchester Police, Strathclyde Police and the Police Service of Northern Ireland, to the smaller, 'shire' forces, such as Dorset or Derbyshire, to others who have a large geographical area, but a relatively small number of officers, such as North Wales Police, Cumbria Constabulary or Scotland's Northern Constabulary.

Home Office
At the head of the structure of this part of the police service, is the Home Office with it's police department, part of the government with a portfolio carried by the current Home Secretary, who is an elected MP and cabinet member. In the election of 2001, David Blunkett replaced Jack Straw, who had been Home Secretary for the first four years of the New Labour government. Under him are various ministers at senior and junior level, and, of course, a large number of permanent staff (non-political, civil servants).

The answerability of the Home Office (via the Home Secretary) to the general public ensures that the notion of 'policing by consent' is maintained in the broad national sense. It is the Home Office that, through parliament, makes (or repeals) laws, and gives powers to the police to ensure they have the required legal basis for the policing of the country.

Police Authorities
To maintain the same accountability at a local level is also important, as there are many variations across the country, from one force area to another, in the demands made of forces and in the way that the public wish to be policed. To do this, there are independent police authorities for each force. They consist of two thirds locally elected councillors and one-third magistrates, ensuring that the interests of the local communities are represented.

The authority for the Metropolitan Police is a relatively new 23-member body. It draws its members from the London Assembly, a member from the district councils outside London and independent members appointed by the Home Secretary.

Many members of Police Authorities are locally elected members who communicate the priorities of their community in their forces' annual policing plan. This plan lays down the objectives and sets targets for the police force to achieve. Additionally the government informs the police of its priorities in the Home Secretary's annual key objectives and ministerial priorities. The Chief Officers have operational control of their resources to meet these priorities and report back to their residents and local and central government via their annual report. The annual report contains information about the progress the Force has achieved and areas for further improvements. Most Forces have attempted to improve the readability and circulation of their reports by producing them in newspaper format and on their Internet websites.

Chief Constable

Each UK police force is led by a Chief Constable, except in London where the Metropolitan Police Service and the City of London police are each commanded by a Commissioner. The Chief Constable is responsible for the management of policing in the area and for overall command of operations that the police carry out on the public's behalf.

The 1964 Police Act established the tri-partite arrangement of control of de-centralised police Forces between the Chief Constable, the Local Authority and the Home Secretary. This ensures a balanced approach to the policing of an area, taking into account the direction of central government, local need and operational responsibility. Whilst it is the responsibility of the Chief Constable to deliver the service, it is also the responsibility of the Home Office and the police authority to facilitate that by providing adequate funding etc. Effectively, all three parts of the triangle must 'manage' up, down and sideways. The people of the UK are ultimately the boss and the customer!

Crime and Disorder Act 1998.

For some time, the police have been working with other agencies, such as local councils, schools and social services, to try to reduce the levels of crime and to increase the security and safety of the public. Also, the Government has made a commitment on tackling crime and the causes of crime. With this in mind the government brought in the Crime and Disorder Act 1998, parts of which create a statutory framework of responsibility and partnership, between local authorities (as opposed to police authorities) and the police, to tackle local issues of crime and public disorder.

It is the responsibility, jointly and equally, of both the local authority and the police force for the area of that local authority, to create strategies to reduce crime and disorder. They are obliged to co-operate together and to act in line with the policing objectives (policing plans) of the relevant police authority. They must additionally co-operate with any probation committee and health authority covering the area.

The Home Secretary may also make specific orders for them to liase with other agencies, groups or individuals, when forming strategies. Thus local accountability and closeness to the needs of the community are further enhanced.

A crime and disorder audit is required to assist partnerships establish their strategic priorities. Skilled staff that understand the policy process and are able to collate and analyse a wide variety of local data on crime and disorder, not simply the crime rates, undertakes audits. Apart from police sources of data on crimes and criminals the local authorities have valuable information on the nature, distribution and costs of crime and disorder not available to the police.

Funding

The fifty-two Police Forces of the United Kingdom are funded by the government and local councils (via the police authorities). The government provides fifty-one per cent of a force budget. This ensures financial accountability across the board.

Non-Geographic Police Forces

Apart from the police forces for areas of the United Kingdom, there are other police forces whose function is to 'police' specific areas that are not necessarily public or geographically defined.

The National Crime Squad
The NCS was formed from an amalgamation of the long established and evolving Regional Crime Squads. These were set up to combat the criminals and their organised crimes, as they increasingly crossed force boundaries. Modern organised crime is run evermore nationally and internationally. The NCS targets and seeks out the major players in organised crime, most of which revolves around drug trafficking.

It is run similarly to a police force, headed by a Director General, with an Assistant Chief Constable running each of the three areas; Northern, Western and Eastern. The Squad is funded by levies paid by all the other forces, and also has its own 'police authority'.

British Transport Police
The BTP covers the rail infrastructure of the country, including the London Underground and the Docklands Light Railway. As well as policing the travelling public they are the lead investigating authority at rail disasters such as the Paddington crash. Their statutory area is within one mile of any railway or station.

They have the same rank structure, with similar responsibilities for each, and the same uniform and equipment as the 'Home Office forces'. They carry out the same functions in relation to crime, disorder and other policing issues. Their training is similar, although they must have additional knowledge and expertise in the function and running of the rail network and in issues of train and railway safety.

United Kingdom Atomic Energy Authority Constabulary
The UKAEAC protects and polices the assets of the nuclear energy industry, encompassing the UKAEA, British Nuclear Fuels PLC and URENCO, both their fixed installations and nuclear products in transit.

The Ministry of Defence Police
The MDP are responsible for the policing and guarding of all military installations and bases in the UK. They work closely with the 'military police forces' of the three armed services. Their areas will include the 'married quarter' estates, which are often 'off site', though ancillary to bases. They also have some responsibility for the security or protection of munitions factories.

The MDP are funded and directed by the Ministry of Defence, though again, their rank structure and uniform is the same as the civil police, as is much of their training. Their statutory area is that of the military areas they cover.

Many of their functions have, in recent years, been reduced and their officers replaced by Ministry of Defence security guards.

Royal Military Police
The RMP is the police force of the Army, policing the army both at home and abroad, both during peacetime and when at war. They also provide 'protection' personnel for military personnel rated by the MOD as needing it.

Royal Naval Regulating Branch
The RN Regulating Branch are the police of the Royal Navy. They provide a policing service on board ships and on British naval bases worldwide. They also often patrol alongside the UK or for-

eign police forces in port towns, where there may be large numbers of naval personnel ashore.

Royal Marines Police
As for the Royal Military Police and Royal Navy Regulators, but specifically for the corps of the Royal Marines.

Royal Air Force Police
The RAFP are the police for the Royal Air Force; their role is again the same as for the police services of the other arms of the British Forces.

The Police of each arm of the Forces have jurisdiction across all three arms, thus all may work together or for each other. 'Officers' are members of that service, and their ranks and structures are those of the armed forces and are not similar to the civil or MOD police.

Port, Waterways, Tunnel and Airport Police
These are a collection of small police forces that cover the areas of various docks, harbours and airports, and also the inland waterways of Great Britain. Officers of these forces are not true police officers in the usual sense but are often sworn into the office of 'constable' by local magistrates, thus gaining many of the statutory powers of the UK Police Service officers. Most operate as officials of the authority, e.g. British Waterways patrol units, who are comprised only of ex-police officers. Their job is to uphold the byelaws associated with their organisation.

Royal Parks Constabulary, Royal Botanic Gardens Constabulary and Borough Parks Police
These forces police the areas of a large number of the major public parks in England and Scotland, including St. James's Park, Kew Gardens and Epping Forest. Again many are park wardens or keepers, sworn in as constables.

The Service Structure

Police Forces
There are currently fifty-two territorial police forces in the United Kingdom. There are thirty-nine in England, eight in Scotland, four in Wales and of course the PSNI in Northern Ireland.

There are about 125,000 police officers, which equates to around one officer for four hundred people. Clearly though, not all of these officers are patrol officers, and only a fraction of those that are, are on duty and on patrol at any one time.

There are also the forces of the Isle of Man, and the States of Jersey and Guernsey. Although not strictly part of the UK, their officers train at UK training centres and their roles and structures are the same.

Police Divisions
To enable the police to cater for local needs and to effectively manage resources under a command structure, each Force is broken down into divisions, each under the leadership of a Superintendent. Divisions are also called Basic Command Units or Operational Command Units. Divisional headquarters may control a network of smaller satellite stations to deliver police services. In addition to uniform officers, stations also have their own CID officers. Cell blocks (custody suites) are provided at main police stations. Call centres and communication rooms are often

situated centrally or in area control rooms and may cover more than one division.
An operations division often supports those divisions responsible for geographic areas. These operations divisions will run those specialised branches which are most effectively commanded from the centre, such as motorway, air support, firearms, dog handlers, search units, mounted branch and force (not divisional) control rooms.

(The Metropolitan Police's ground is divided into eight 'areas', each, in terms of population, about the size of a provincial force. These areas are then sub-divided into divisions.)

In line with the theme of local accountability and response to local needs, the government driven system of sector policing is now prevalent. Each division will have a number of sectors based on the topography of the territory. A group of local officers known as a 'community action team' manages the liaison between local communities - through local councillors - and the police.

The Police Station

The traditional red brick police station of the late Victorian era was a symbol of power and an edifice normally situated prominently in the centre of a town. Periods of modernisation, for example during the 1960s, replaced many of these buildings with more up to date stations.

As most public contact with the police is by telephone, and in some ways the Internet, the value of a building with all departments being under one roof is declining. In the same way as department stores find difficulty competing with more specialised out of town retailers, the police station of the future is set to look radically different as functions are hived off.

Purpose built centralised custody centres, also called main bridewells, can process detainees efficiently and economically. The support provided in modern and well-staffed facilities also reduces the likelihood of prisoners committing self-harm. This concept can, however, create logistical problems of time spent in transit, with officers away from their area for longer periods. There are also difficulties in terms of human rights, when a detainee is released, perhaps many miles from home and with no means of getting there.

Call handling and command and control centres are more likely to be built away from traditional police stations and in future they may also act as multi-agency centres combining the other emergency services, local authorities and even utilities, such as water, gas and electricity. The concept is to provide a 'one-stop-shop' for members of the public who telephone for advice, support and assistance.

All this leaves the police station with is office space for administrative functions and a place in which to book on and off duty. These functions can be easily and more cheaply conducted in low cost rented office accommodation on the outskirts of towns. It is possible for rented office space to accommodate the administrative functions. Under private finance initiatives commercial enterprises may bid to run support functions. There will still be a need for a point of contact for members of the public to interact with the police services. This could be a 'cop shop' store front in the town centre, an electronic public information point or even part of a local post office that is dedicated to provide information about police services.

However, the undoubted 'comfort' of having a local police station, with most things under one roof, providing a secure environment, with everything handy for it's staff and the public, is of tremendous morale value.

The Ranks

The Office of Constable

For most people uniformed Police Constables are 'The Police'. It is the entry rank for all new recruits; it is the rank in which officers serve longest. The majority of police officers are constables and constables have the majority of contact with the public. In short, they are the backbone of the service.

Constables deliver service to the public through high visibility patrolling, attending incidents, giving advice and support, quelling disturbances, reassuring the community, intercepting and arresting criminals. These officers need to be omni-competent. It is a most demanding and rewarding job.

To create a police service that reflects the community it serves, forces encourage women and people from ethnic minority communities to apply for jobs. In Northern Ireland, where Catholics have been underrepresented in the Police Service of Northern Ireland, efforts are being made to increase their numbers. As positive discrimination is not lawful, all applicants must satisfy the entry requirements of the selection procedure regardless of gender, ethnicity, sexual orientation or any other factor that is not related to the safe and effective performance of the job.

Sergeants

Uniformed police sergeants on Divisions are the first tier of management. This means that the performance and development of their officers is of great importance.

A patrol sergeant leads a group of officers, from a handful to a dozen or more depending on their area and reports to an Inspector. Sergeants ensure that the officers attend incidents and tackle local problems. They also perform the role of control room supervisors, ensuring that the operators create computer based incident reports and despatch resources appropriately.

Another demanding job for a Sergeant is that of Custody Officer. The Custody Officer is responsible for supervising the detention of prisoners, ensuring that their rights are respected and that they are processed without delay, all in accordance with the Police and Criminal Evidence Act 1984, and it's various updates, which govern the detention and questioning of suspects.

Detective Sergeants work in plain clothes normally in the CID and lead a team of Detectives to tackle local crime. They will direct their officers to investigate crimes that have been committed and to identify crime hot-spot locations or active criminals.

Inspector

A uniformed Inspector at Divisional level could be placed in charge of a group of Sergeants and PCs, collectively called a relief, block, section or rota. Alternatively the Inspector could be tasked with overseeing the policing of a geographical area within a division - a sector. Apart from leading the response to serious incidents, such as disasters and firearms situations, Police Inspectors have statutory responsibilities for reviewing prisoners, taking complaints and conducting identity parades.

Detective Inspectors in the CID will report to their Detective Chief Inspector, often referred to as a Crime Manager. They are responsible for the performance of their Detective Sergeants and Detective Constables as they tackle local crime problems. DIs may also have other specialised roles, such as hostage negotiator.

Chief Inspector

The uniformed Chief Inspector on a Division could be in charge of Human Resources, i.e. personnel and training issues. It is common for them to be in charge of police operations. One of the main functions of the Chief Inspector is to deputise for the Superintendent.

The Detective Chief Inspector, or Crime Manager, reports to the Divisional Superintendent on their team's performance in tackling crime. DCIs and DIs are often specially trained to be Senior Investigating Officers who lead the response to major crimes, such as murders, or big frauds or robberies.

Superintendent

The Divisional Superintendent is responsible for the overall performance of the police in his or her area, both uniform and CID. The Superintendent will ensure that the local business plan reflects local needs and ensure that the officers achieve performance targets.

Superintendents still have an operational role as they can command the response to major incidents and perform statutory responsibilities, e.g. by authorising extensions to prisoners' detention, or intimate searches of detained persons under certain circumstances.

Senior Officers

Officers above the rank of Superintendent, that is Chief Superintendent, assistant Chief Constable and Deputy Chief Constable, often have force-wide thematic responsibilities, such as crime, operations and discipline. Increasingly, a senior civilian, rather than a police officer, now does the specialised work involved in finance.

In consultation with the police authority and central government, senior officers set out the strategic mission for their force, which will become embodied in the 'corporate plan'. This is translated down to more focused action plans and targets in the Divisional business plans. These in turn can break down into sector initiatives and objectives. The results are then analysed and fed back up to senior level for assessment of effectiveness.

Special Constabulary

Special constables are unpaid volunteers who devote a few hours a week of their spare time to assist their local police force. As well as training and equipment the Specials are also given full police powers. They form a vital link between the regular police and the local community.

A worrying trend nationally is that Specials are leaving faster than they can be recruited, many citing dissatisfaction with their supervision, training and deployment. To retain these valued members Forces need to improve the experience of being a Special and reduce the wastage rate. Successive administrations have attempted to recruit more Specials as it fits with the concept of the 'active citizen'. It also provides a welcome boost to the numbers of uniformed officers on the streets and helps to reassure the public. One important factor in retaining Specials is the support they receive from their employer.

Support Staff

The Police today would find it difficult, if not impossible, to function without the valuable support provided by its civilian staff members.

The support staff have traditionally been used in administrative functions to release officers for operational duties. This still occurs with civilians supporting the organisation from cleaning, catering, security and clerical work right up to senior officer level. More and more civilians are being used to interact with the public and assist in investigations. There are also aircraft pilots, traffic wardens, detention officers, front desk officers, and crime scene examiners.

Staff Associations

ACPO and ACPOS
The two main associations for chief police officers are the Association of Chief Police Officers of England, Wales and Northern Ireland (ACPO) and the Association of Chief Police Officers of Scotland (ACPOS). Their members represent Assistant Chief Constables, Deputy Chief Constables and Chief Constables.

ACPO has sub-committees dedicated to thematic areas of policing such at Information Technology, Firearms and Arrest, Restraint and Self-Defence. Each sub-committee explores strategic level issues on their remit and makes sure that good practice is recommended to Forces.

Superintendents' Association
The Superintendents' Association encourages better police management and represents its members. With the reduction in the numbers of superintending ranks, Superintendents and Chief Superintendents face an ever-increasing workload. Legislation such as the Health and Safety at Work Act, places even more responsibility on their shoulders.

Police Federation
The Police Federation represents the interests of officers from Police Constable to Chief Inspector, the 'Federated Ranks'. Created in the aftermath of the police strike at the end of the First World War, this staff association does not have any recourse to call for industrial action, as it is illegal for police officers to withdraw their labour and it is also an offence to incite them to strike. However, in most other respects it is the ordinary police officer's 'union'.

UNISON
UNISON is the trade union representing the civilian members whose support is vital to the running of the police.

Other Associations
There are other groups that serving officers may join or be represented by, such as the British Association of Women Police, the Lesbian and Gay Police Association and the National Black Police Association. These groups provide an additional support network for their members to encourage them to continue serving in the police despite the pressures that can occur from being in a minority in the organisation.

National Police Organisations
Non-geographic police forces, such as the British Transport Police and UK Atomic Energy Authority Constabulary, have arrangements between their chief officers and their regulating authorities.

CHAPTER 3. INVESTIGATING CRIME AND CRIMINALS

Whilst the detection of crime remains one of the core activities for all police officers, a huge part of any police force, is its teams of detectives, be they part of the re-active CID (Criminal Investigation Department), pro-active squads, drug squads, vehicle crime squads, vice squads, the National Crime Squad and its regional offices and many others, whose job is specifically to investigate crime and criminals. Roughly one in eight of all police officers are on the CID or a specialist or centralised crime- fighting team.

Although this has the public view of being the glamorous side of the job, it is the hours, days or even years of painstaking evidence gathering and sifting and the meticulous preparation of evidence and case files that are the reality.

For every type of prolific crime or any particularly active team of criminals, there will be a team or squad of officers dedicated to the prevention and detection of the offences being committed.

Organised crime is increasingly a problem. In August 2001, the National Crime Intelligence Service (NCIS) admitted it was struggling in the fight against some eight hundred organised gangs who were bringing hard drugs into the country. Most forces have some form of 'serious crime squad' or 'major crime unit' to deal with this.

Bearing the main burden will be the CID of each division or sub-division, under the leadership of a crime manager. These are the officers who, as trained detectives, investigate the vast majority of those crimes not dealt with by the uniform patrol officers. They will invariably be the first detectives at the scene of a crime, even if it is subsequently passed on to a specialist team.

Pro-active teams look at crime trends, or individual criminals or teams of criminals who may be active in the area. Making good use of surveillance and intelligence, they will aim to be one step ahead and therefore able to prevent crimes even happening, or to catch criminals 'red-handed'.

The Specialists
To deal with specific crimes, some CID officers are specially trained and may form specialist teams from local or force level, up to regional or national level. Many female and some male officers are trained to deal with offences of rape or serious sexual assault. Others are trained in dealing with children, some of whom, as victims, may be very young indeed.

As mentioned above, the problem of illegal drug supply is big. Drug squads nationwide use the very latest methods of surveilling and catching the dealers, often working closely with other agencies such as HM Customs and Excise, or even the armed forces.

The National Football Intelligence Unit, targets the widespread problem of organised football hooliganism. Its officers will often travel abroad and liase closely with similar units in other countries.

There are specialists in 'white-collar' crime - fraud squads dedicated to tackling business swindles, major credit card fraud and keeping bang up to date, computer based crime. The process of gathering and presenting evidence in such cases is highly complex, lengthy and demanding. The huge sums of money or numbers of victims, which can be subject of one criminal operation, however, justify the effort. The Fraud Squad, run jointly by the Metropolitan Police and the City of London Police, is the national team for this type of crime. Officers from both forces also work within the Serious Fraud Office, which is a government department, set up as a result of the Criminal Justice Act of 1987, to investigate and prosecute serious crime of this nature.

The Metropolitan Police has an anti-terrorist squad. London has historically been the foremost, though certainly not the only, target for terrorists in the UK, outside Northern Ireland. Incidents outside the Metropolitan area may also be attended by officers from the anti-terrorist squad, who will have specific skills and knowledge, useful in any co-ordinated action or investigation.

With the terrorist attacks of September 2001 in America, sending shock waves across the world, resulting in the declaration of 'war' against terrorism; the work of the anti-terrorist unit and indeed all the police in this field, will only intensify.

Whatever the crime, there will be someone dedicated to fighting it. If the criminal fraternity think of something new, the police will not be far behind.

'Intelligence led' policing is one of the main thrusts in the fight against crime. Local, regional and national bureaus of intelligence, sift through mountains of sometimes obscure snippets of intelligence. Sometimes this will be gained after months of dedicated surveillance, or from just a brief report by a uniform patrol officer, who has noted something that may be of interest to someone, somewhere.

The National Criminal Intelligence Service (NCIS) is the umbrella organisation and has the role of co-ordinating intelligence from all the main agencies. The National Crime Squad, HM Customs and Excise, MI5 (The Security Service) and MI6 (The Secret Intelligence Service) must all report to NCIS.

A recent report by Lord Spedding criticised the various agencies for not communicating with each other sufficiently, suggesting some jealous guarding of intelligence gained through their own networks. This has been seen to be a factor in a lack of success in the fight against major organised crime. With NCIS now officially 'in charge' it is hoped that better and faster links and an ethos of intelligence sharing will vastly improve success.

Special Branch
The Special Branch was created in 1883. It was originally called the Special Irish Branch set up to counter the activities of Fenian bombers who had targeted London. It was and remains a largely intelligence based section of a force. However, whilst the threat from the

IRA and other Northern Ireland groups remains, the remit of a force' Special Branch is nowadays much wider. Generally it is there to gather and hold high-level intelligence on the nefarious or seditious activities of any individual or group. It links closely with MI5 and MI6.

Now that the Terrorism Act 2000 includes such groups as animal rights activists, anti-capitalism anarchists and others who may use criminal methods to achieve their aims, Special Branch officers must have in-depth knowledge of current affairs and the motives of such people. New and more robust legislation will no doubt result from the destruction of the New York World Trade Center, as the world generally becomes aware of the scale of international terrorism and resolve strengthens to fight it.

The Special Branch provides threat assessments for events and prominent people such as politicians or visiting dignitaries. Many forces have authorised firearms officers on their Special Branch, who provide protection for any people deemed to be under a generic or specific threat.

SOCO
One of the most important parts of the investigation of a crime is the preservation of the crime scene. This is so that vital photographic evidence, fingerprints, footmarks, fibres, blood and, more recently, DNA can be preserved in the way it was left by the suspects.

It falls upon all officers, even the victim or person reporting the crime or discovery of something to try not to disturb anything. It is the job of the Scenes Of Crime Officer (SOCO) to find and 'lift' the evidence and take the photographs. SOCO will have the ability to remove all manner of things for subsequent forensic scientific examination.

Suspects who are arrested for crimes, have for many years, had to give their fingerprints and have their photograph taken. They now have to give samples of DNA from a mouth swab. This is analysed for a DNA profile that is stored on a national computer database. DNA found at the scene of a crime is compared to the profiles on the database to find a match. So good is this method of identification that crimes committed long ago, but never solved, have now been detected as a result of the taking of DNA from hair samples or body fluid taken at the time.

SOCOs are nowadays mostly civilian staff, who may already possess skills in areas like photography.

There are more SOCOs now than ever before. As new scientific techniques are found, there is more work for them to do. The Courts too are more ready to accept scientific evidence as its reliability has improved.

Crime Prevention
There is the well-known saying, 'prevention is better than cure'. All forces have 'Crime Prevention Officers' (CPOs). Their job is to look at ways of making things harder or impossible for the criminal. They may give advice to a householder on types of alarms or

locks to fit. Shops may benefit from advice regarding shop layout, CCTV, or forged note detectors. Car owners will be shown the best immobilisation or tracking devices, or better places to leave the car, with less in it. This may only have the effect of making the criminal go and commit crime elsewhere, rather than not at all, a phenomenon known as 'crime displacement'. Still, anything that makes life tougher for criminals has to be a good thing.

The initial design and layout of new housing estates is one area where early involvement of the CPO may avoid future problems. Most are available to give advice freely if asked for. A visit from the CPO may stem from a premises being repeatedly targeted by criminals.

CHAPTER 4. SPECIALIST UNIFORMED OPERATIONS

Police officers are generally very well skilled in a large number of areas. As the 'basic bobby on the beat', an officer will have to deal with everything and anything. But as with crime fighting, where the various 'plain clothes' people will be called in initially or in support, there are numerous areas where uniformed officers are required who have specialised in certain areas and have been trained in additional skills or to a very high level. The most familiar and whose activities are perhaps the most controversial at times, are of course traffic officers and, increasingly, firearms officers. But there are many other specialists who rarely make any headlines, but whose work is indispensable in the modern police service.

Traffic

This is the specialist job that, aside from CID, has the largest number of officers. They are easily identifiable by their white caps.

Traffic officers are trained to an advanced level of driving, usually requiring to be to Grade 1 Advanced level, thus they are trained to drive high powered cars safely and quickly in response to emergency calls, or in pursuit situations. (See also Chapter 5- Operational Policing). Many are also trained as police motorcyclists. Some officers are further trained to drive heavy goods vehicles or buses and coaches - PSVs. Whereas in general any member of the public can drive any car with just a car licence, the rules set for police officers as to what level of training is required for what type of police car, driven under what circumstances, vary from force to force.

Primarily, traffic officers enforce road traffic law, and many forces have special centralised teams who do just that, targeting accident spots or mounting operations in response to specific complaints of congestion or driving behaviour. Leaving the reactive side, such as attending accidents or responding to spontaneous calls from the public, to divisional traffic departments.

Currently it falls to the police to 'escort' abnormal or wide loads. This is one area that may well become the sole responsibility of the haulage company that will have to provide it's own trained people. It will doubtless remain that permission to move particular loads at certain times will still be obtained from the police.

Dealing with road traffic collisions is one of the most stressful jobs an officer can do. The chaos, damage, injuries and trauma that they may have to deal with can be horrific. Some officers specialise in accident investigation. In the event of a serious or fatal collision, these accident investigation officers will piece together all the evidence from witnesses and drivers. They will also examine the wreckage and the road surface, to work out how fast the vehicles were going and exactly where they were when they collided. In any resultant prosecution or inquest, their evidence will be vital.

Firearms Officers

All forces have specialist firearms officers, trained in the use of firearms to be deployed to resolve critical incidents where they may have to face someone who is armed, or is otherwise so dangerous that that person could not be safely restrained by any other means. The 'use' of a firearm by a police officer does not mean firing it. It means having it ready to use only as a last resort. The mere presence of armed officers is usually enough to resolve a situation without anyone being harmed.

Training differs from force to force and the level to which officers are trained also varies. Some forces give a basic two weeks training (as per the ACPO manual of guidance, drawn up after the Waldorf shooting in London) to officers who crew armed response vehicles, with more training for the tactical firearms teams, whilst others train all their officers to a high level, up to eight weeks before being qualified, irrespective of their particular firearms role.

The highest profile firearms officers are those of the armed response units. These provide an immediate armed response to incidents involving firearms. Generally their job is to contain the situation until more armed teams can be deployed, but as the depth and quality of training increases, there are more incidents that can be resolved by the initial response team, without calling out further staff.

There are also specialist roles that some firearms officers train for.

Rifle officer (sniper) - these officers are trained to use long-range highly accurate rifles, usually 7.62mm calibre. They are also trained in the skills required for covert observations and operations, including camouflage and concealment.

Protection Officer - trained as armed 'body guards', these officers are used to protect VIPs, such as the Royal Family, the Prime Minister and various members of parliament or cabinet members. They may also be required to protect witnesses, or people who are under threat (the author Salman Rushdie being one example). The Metropolitan Police have an entire branch devoted to this work, the Royalty and Diplomatic Protection Branch.

Rapid Intervention (or Dynamic Entry) - Specialists trained to be the last resort in a situation which now requires a rapid and decisive entry to a building or perhaps an aircraft, in a siege or hostage situation, where lives are in immediate danger. They are trained in abseiling and techniques to effect entry through locked doors or even walls!
This is a role developed after the famous Iranian Embassy siege of 1981, which was ended by an SAS entry. The army have relinquished this role in all but the most extreme situations with an international involvement, in order to concentrate on their 'normal' job. The Police have now developed and become expert in this field.

In any firearms incident, the final decision to shoot or not shoot, rests entirely on the officer pulling the trigger and his or her perception of the threat presented. Any officer making the decision to fire becomes automatically the subject of a thorough investigation, along with the rest of the team and all commanders at every level involved in the incident. This is carried out by the Police Complaints Authority, and is routine, not an indication that the police have made a mistake.

So far in the United Kingdom, police officers have not been routinely armed, other than in Northern Ireland. Even if it were necessary, it would be very difficult to maintain the high standards of selection and training currently enjoyed, if all officers had to be armed. However, provided that that standard is maintained and that the existing armed officers are deployed effectively, the day that all officers are armed in this country should not arrive.

Search Teams

The definition of 'searching' in the police is a very broad one. For everything that the police may have to find, from missing people to tiny bits of evidence at either a crime scene or at perhaps the scene of a major accident, there are officers highly trained in the techniques of searching.

Missing persons

Search officers coordinated by POLSAs (Police Search Advisors) will lead the search for missing people such as young children or other vulnerable persons. Patterns of searching will be devised according to the background of the person, the type of area, weather conditions and the circumstances of the disappearance. The Police search officers will also coordinate any multi-agency approach such as with mountain or cave rescue teams, the military or local volunteers.

Evidence

Most people will be familiar with the news images of lines of officers making fingertip searches along roads or hedgerows, particularly after bomb explosions or where missing children have been last seen. They will be looking for tiny clues, bits of clothing or fragments of an explosive device.

Search officers will also be used to find evidence of, or stolen goods from, crime, either at the scene or the home or business premises of the suspect. They will often work closely with dogs and have a vast array of special equipment.

Pre-visit Searching

In the same way as many VIPs are protected by police protection officers, so too must the areas they are going to be made safe. If there is a publicised event to take place, involving the attendance of a VIP who may be generically or specifically under threat, then the venue must be clear prior to the arrival of the VIP. This may involve searching and sealing manholes and drain covers, searching all the rooms of a venue and then keeping it 'sterile' by searching all people who subsequently enter. For something like a theatre or hotel, and the street along which the VIP must arrive, this can take many hours of searching by large numbers of officers and dogs.

The Metropolitan Police has its own bomb disposal team, whereas other forces utilise and work closely with, the Explosive Ordnance Disposal (EOD) teams from the army, who are based around the country.

Underwater Search Units

Police divers do much the same work as the search officers described above, but obviously their work is searching underwater. Most forces share an underwater search unit with others in their region. Divers are trained at one of two national schools in Northumberland (Northumbria Police) and Hampshire.

Despite the somewhat glamorous sound to the title, the job mostly involves swimming or wading through rivers, canals or sewers, looking for dead bodies or other evidence that may have been there for a long time.

They are also invaluable in searching hulls of ships in harbour, that may have been used for smuggling drugs.

Dog Handlers

One of the most important tools in the police service is the police dog, and there are many and various roles for dogs and their handlers.

Dogs are teamed up with their handlers at a very young age, normally between eight and eighteen months, and the training is thorough and demanding. Only the best will do.

The main 'all rounder' will be the familiar German Shepherd. These have proven to be strong, faithful and courageous animals. They have good ability in tracking and searching, with the added bonus of being large and loud, excellent if needed in situations of disorder, or to tackle a dangerous individual.

Police dogs of other breeds, e.g. spaniels, are becoming increasingly useful as specialist 'sniffer' dogs. They are trained to detect all manner of things, such as explosives, drugs and firearms, or to find people trapped in wreckage or rubble. Even buried bodies. They may also be particularly good at tracking, which is necessary when searching for missing people or for criminals on the run.

It is becoming more common now for handlers to have two dogs, a general one like the German Shepherd, and another specialist dog. Some handlers work with firearms teams, with the dog being familiar with the appearance and smell of guns and firearms officers, and the way in which the teams work. Those handlers with specialist 'sniffer' or 'tracker' dogs will be trained in the particular methods required to deploy such animals and will have expert knowledge in, for example, the methods used by criminals to hide drugs.

Research is continually underway to establish what breeds are best at what.

Police Support Units (PSUs)

PSUs are colloquially known as the riot squads. Unfortunately they are becoming an increasingly familiar sight around the country. After the numerous inner-city summer riots of 1981, and the conflict of the miner's strikes in 1984, the police looked hard at the training and equipment it had to respond to situations of serious public disorder. As a result, PSU trained officers have good equipment and training, to protect them in robustly dealing with rioting. Gone are the days of merely pulling down the chinstrap of a standard police helmet. Officers now have fire retardant overalls, armour, full helmets with visors, and disciplined tactics to cope with the fluidity of a public disorder incident.

Police Support Unit Officer

1. Helmet
2. Anti-flash hood
3. Fire retardant overalls
4. Kevlar lined gloves (with Kevlar sleeves under overalls)
5. Fire extinguisher
6. Belt and shoulder rig with baton, handcuffs and radio
7. Elbow and forearm shields
8. Knee and leg shields
9. Protective boots with steel toe caps

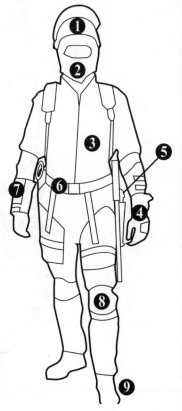

Photo by Alan Roberts

Armed Response Vehicle

1. Ballistic short shield
2. Ballistic long shield with window
3. Ceramic high velocity shield panel
4. Remington repeater 12g shotgun
5. Heckler and Koch MP5 9mm carbines
6. Glock 17 9mm self loading pistols

7. CASCO expandable batons
8. Hand lamp with infra-red filter
9. Infra-red image monocular
10. Binoculars
11. Ballistic helmets
12. Tactical equipment vest
13. Medic pack with oxygen

14. Vehicle immobiliser spikes
15. Polaroid camera
16. Respirator (gas mask)
17. Kevlar long-sleeved gloves
18. Ballistic blanket
19. Loading/unloading bag
20. Volvo V70 T-5 estate car

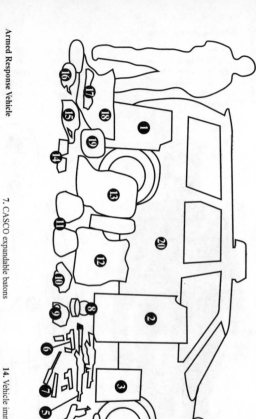

33

Mounted Police

Most of the big city forces, the Metropolitan Police in London, Greater Manchester Police, Merseyside and Strathclyde amongst others, have a mounted section.

Although very expensive, officers on horses have proved valuable in crowd control situations such as at football matches. The high visible presence and weight of the horse itself contributes to effective control. In some places, mounted officers are used to police town or city centres where vehicle access may be difficult.

They are also used for policing those big royal parades where the army and all the VIPs may be using horses or horse drawn carriages.

As with dogs, only the very best horses will be good enough and their training, and that of their riders, is again, long and thorough.

Air Support Units
(See Chapter 11. Aviation)`

CHAPTER 5. CURRENT POLICING ISSUES

This Chapter covers a selection of the challenges facing the police today.

Potential Overload

As there are few areas of activity in society where the police could not have a legitimate professional interest there is a real danger of them becoming overloaded with demands for their limited resources. The list of new demands includes illegal immigration, environmental pollution, the protection of endangered species and cyber-crime.

New technology can bring with it more problems for the police. Emergency 999 calls are increasing, partly due to false calls being accidentally dialled on mobile phones. The general level of calls for service has increased significantly in most forces. This may also be due to the ease of access through increased telephone ownership. There is an increased expectation of rapid attendance to a call, perhaps part of a general rise in the perception of 'consumer power' being extended to the police by an optimistic public. Exaggeration is now more frequent than before. Someone reporting an incident is likely to 'add' to the urgency of the call, in anticipation of a higher prioritisation and a quicker, more robust, response.

Performance Culture

Previous attempts at improving performance in the public sector have attempted to replicate the discipline of the economy by creating artificial internal markets. It was hoped that this would deliver efficiencies, as only the most efficient sections would succeed.

Another option is to focus on target setting and establishing quantitative performance figures. It is used extensively in the business planning process. In this way performance can be measured and organisations can be compared, by placing them in league tables and, in the most extreme cases, by publicly 'naming and shaming'. A victim of crime wants the police to attend in a certain length of time (quantitative), but more importantly wants to receive a professional caring level of service (qualitative).

It is predicted that this performance culture will continue and mature. Advances in measuring qualitative performance will be made. Police forces will strive to improve their performance to meet targets. Sometimes this will be achieved with fewer resources; the often quoted phrase, "Doing more, with less."

Joined up Policing

Signs of closer international co-operation between law enforcement agencies can be seen; especially where open borders allow virtually unrestricted passage. The challenge facing the police is to permit the free flow of the law-abiding majority and the interception of criminals (especially drug traffickers and since September, 2001 terrorists) and illegal immigrants. This can only be done effectively with full co-operation on an international scale - joined up policing.

Advances in technology have led to a worrying rise in cyber-crime making some current laws and existing police boundaries less relevant. When a single virus, the "I love you" bug, can cause billions of pounds of damage to companies across the globe one can appreciate the scale of the threat to society.

The police are expected to close this gap between them and this new area of criminal activity. This will be achieved by increasing the police expertise in the field, co-operation with other agencies, and changes in legislation.

Stop & Search
Police powers to stop and search people, who are suspected of carrying stolen or prohibited articles (offensive weapons or things used to commit various crimes), are vital tools in combating crime.

Critics point to the fact that about nine out of ten stop checks are unsuccessful and, more importantly, they disproportionately affect members of ethnic minorities. This has been used to support the police being labelled as institutionally racist.

Community and race relations training assists police officers in acting impartially. This area has been studied and some suggestions have been put forward as to why this disparity exists. It is espoused that some officers may feel that they are more likely to make a written record of stop checks on ethnic minority persons in case they are challenged later. If correct, this may account for the disproportionate number of stop checks on blacks and Asians.

Whatever the reason, stop and search monitoring will continue to be a high priority to ensure that police powers are exercised objectively, reasonably and proportionately.

Working with the Community
Police acceptance of sole responsibility for the level of crime is unrealistic. Crime is a complex, society-wide problem. The most effective way of tackling crime is through working in partnership with community agencies. Indeed, this is what the Crime and Disorder Act 1998 demands. Crime reduction projects involve the police and local authorities. Partnerships are in early stage of development and there are still challenges to be overcome such as sharing information that require data protection protocols. To make the partnership effective it needs resources allocating to it, e.g., full-time rather than part-time. It needs dynamic application with short-term projects and dissemination of good practice to others.

When tackling crime the multi-agency approach is not one way ahead, it is the only way ahead.

Best Value
Best Value is a challenging Government initiative that establishes a performance framework for the police and other local authorities. It is defined as, 'a duty to deliver services to clear standards, covering both cost and quality, by the most effective, economic and efficient means available.' The responsibility of the police (and other local providers of services) is

the local residents who pay for their services.

In the Best Value process the police fundamentally review their aims and objectives; the nature of the local needs; their ability to satisfy these needs; and, the resources available.

Best Value is a back to basics initiative that modernises the police through reviewing the way decisions are made and consulting with the communities they serve. The aim is to make incremental improvements to the services the police provide to their residents through a rolling programme of Fundamental Performance Reviews. The performance of forces is measured against other forces and serious or persistent failure could lead to intervention by the Home Secretary. The key aspects of the Fundamental Performance Reviews are the 4C's:

• Challenge - To question how and why each service is being provided or even if it should be provided at all.
• Compare - To compare the police performance with several measures against other providers of service.
• Consult - To open a dialogue with stakeholders (residents, consumers of service and the business community) about performance targets.
• Compete - To have fair competition to secure efficient and effective services.

This has of course to be balanced by the cost of teams to do this, even smaller forces are having to spend over half a million pounds. Nor does best value always mean cheaper.

Arming the Police
It is a myth that the police are not armed in the United Kingdom. However it is true that the British police are not armed routinely. This is almost unique in the world. (The PSNI, formerly the RUC, is currently routinely armed. Hopefully the need for this will one day be consigned to history).

In the wake of any officer murdered in the line of duty there is often a call for the police to be armed. Whether or not this pressure can be resisted remains to be seen. If it is the police duty to protect the public an unarmed officer cannot effectively do it when faced with an armed criminal until the arrival of armed officers.

If the experience of other police forces is any guide there is likely to be paradoxical rise in the number of shootings of officers if the police are armed. Even if criminals do not arm themselves, officers are likely to be shot after being disarmed in violent confrontations.

Some officers may be reluctant to carry firearms and there would be yet another abstraction from frontline policing due to training.

Officer Safety
For the safety of the public officers may need to get in harms way. Safety is therefore an ever-present issue with police officers.

As an occupation, policing has a high rate of its employees being assaulted. Although there are measures that can be taken to minimise assaults through stringent liquor licensing laws and deterrence through punitive sentences, frontline policing can be a 'hands on' contact employment where assaults are almost inevitable. To counter such attacks, officers are trained to assess and defuse conflict situations. Where such tactics fail they are trained in 'empty-handed' techniques, CS, handcuffs, and batons. Some are also trained with firearms. Many are also issued with protective equipment such as ballistic and stab resistant body armour.

The aim of the equipment and training is the safety of the public by managing the conflict situation and the restoration of order.

Vehicle Pursuit

Of the thousand plus fatalities on the roads each year in collisions a couple of dozen may involve a police pursuit. These deaths receive an understandably large amount of press coverage. Whilst every death is unacceptable and tragic there is obvious concern expressed where the police are involved.

In an effort to minimise the risk of injury or death the police have adopted a raft of measures including policies, training and equipment to make pursuits safer for all concerned, including the police officers.

Advanced courses train officers in the tactics to conclude a pursuit safely. They are also made aware of the concept of 'red mist', where drivers become so focused on arresting the errant driver that they lose their objectivity. Tactics are taught to box in vehicles with a team of other drivers.

Two things have assisted in the safer resolution of pursuit situations, namely road spikes and air support. Hollow spikes can be deployed across the road ahead of a vehicle to deflate the tyres in a controlled manner that will bring the vehicle to a halt, eventually. These spikes allow officers to make a valuable contribution to safely ending a pursuit by setting up a trap rather than joining in a dangerous train of vehicles behind the pursued vehicle. Police aircraft can monitor the pursuit and give a radio commentary to allow officers on the ground to follow at a safe distance, as the air support officers keep the suspects in sight.

As the remit of the police is public safety, considerable media coverage occurs when deaths and serious injuries result from collisions involving police vehicles.

During the 1990's research found that the number of fatal and serious injury collisions peaked in 1993 then declined. The study also found that 88 per cent of those collisions involved the following activities
Pursuit - 45%
Responding to emergencies - 23%
Routine patrol - 20 %

Stolen vehicles were involved in more than a quarter (27 per cent) of collisions.

To reduce the risk of injury or death involved in collisions, the police have a three-pronged approach.

1. Operational issues

Pursuit management. Forces have written policies to minimise the number of pursuits. Police managers can order pursuits to be stopped in certain circumstances. New techniques and equipment make pursuits safer such as tactical pursuit and containment, air support and tyre deflating devices. These may already have changed the nature of pursuits by seeking to bring them to a controlled conclusion.

Sirens and lights.- As some collisions occur when the vehicles are not using lights and sirens it is generally considered to be good practice for them to be used when pursuing or when on an emergency call to warn other road users. There are times where it is counterproductive to use them and not sound tactically.

Mandatory alcohol tests.- It is good practice to rebut any suggestion that the police driver was under the influence of alcohol for him or her to be breath tested following a collision.

2. Training issues

Night-time driving.- As most collisions happen at night, some training is given during the hours of darkness to prepare officers for pursuits in conditions of reduced visibility.

Pursuit training.- Some drivers involved in collisions were not specifically trained for pursuits. There is obviously a need to prevent such officers becoming involved in following a pursuit. A more appropriate use for such general drivers could be to park up and prepare to use tyre deflation equipment. In this way their natural enthusiasm for assisting in the pursuit could be channelled into a safer activity.

3. Administration of collisions

A series of measures are taken to record collisions and driver records to monitor any trends and take control measures.

Despite every precaution collisions will still happen in future. Although there are many issues which the police address to make pursuits safer the responsibility lies with the offending driver. The motorcar cannot become sanctuary for the criminal and the police can be expected to perform their duty to protect the public by stopping dangerous criminals behind the wheel.

Accountability

Policing with the consent of the public is the 'British Police Advantage'. The police need to be accountable to the public. The police are in fact more accountable than most. In addition to being accountable to the criminal law and civil law; officers are subject to the police performance and misconduct procedures. Forces are also scrutinised by the media as well as the Home Office and local consultative forums.

Corrupt officers damage public confidence in their police and has been highlighted by the National Criminal Intelligence Service. For criminals the easiest way to advance their position is to corrupt the police. If the reduction in pay and conditions makes officers more susceptible to corruption then it is a worrying time for the police.

Police Community Consultative Group

The PCCGs stem back from Section 106(1) of the Police and Criminal Evidence Act 1984. 'Arrangements shall be made in each police area for obtaining the views of people in that area about matters concerning the policing of the area, and for obtaining their co-operation with the police in preventing crime in the area.'

The PCCG therefore act as a link between the communities they represent and the official bodies within the framework of the Crime and Disorder Act.

To prevent PCCGs becoming talking shops for professional meeting goers they canvass views of the community through public meetings, working parties, religious groups, neighbourhood watch and housing associations.

Problem-Orientated Policing

Traditional community policing could be characterised by the 3Rs of rapid response, random patrolling and reactive investigation. William Bratton (former head of the New York Police Department and linked with a zero tolerance approach) redefined it as the 3Ps namely partnership, problem solving and prevention.

Problem-Oriented Policing (POP) is being implemented in many parts of the UK to police communities. The concept of POP envisages the police identifying and solving the causes of problems in the community, rather than reacting to individual incidents. POP delivers a better service delivery to the public as their problems are tackled; more job satisfaction for the officers; and, more manageable demands on resources as repeat calls are reduced.

For POP to be effective it needs the commitment from the entire police organisation, rather than the establishment of a small group of officers. It is the officer on the beat who is closest to the community and more in tune with their problems. These officers can deliver POP if they are provided with the right conditions and resources from the organisation, this includes:

• A bottom-up structure that identifies problems as well as solutions.
• Involves as many beat officers as possible.
• Develops a training package for officers.
• Enables experienced local officers to analyse incident patterns.
• Considers multiple problems simultaneously.
• Assesses the impact of every response to problems.
• Involves the public continuously in identifying and responding to problems.

There are two tools that are used in problem solving which use the mnemonics 'SARA and 'PAT'.

SARA stands for:
• Scanning - identifying problem areas.
• Analysis - investigating problems to find their root causes.
• Response - devising solutions through working with the community and bringing in other

agencies.
• Assessment - reviewing the performance.

PAT is the Problem Analysis Triangle. This encourages officers to analyse the problem from three perspectives, the people making the complaint; the place where the problem occurs and, the people being complained about.

Policing Racially Motivated Incidents

The UK prides itself on being a multi-cultural society and is probably one of the most diverse countries in the world. It is essential therefore that everyone should challenge racially motivated incidents. From the figures in this guide it appears that racially motivated incidents have increased significantly. What the figures show, is that the number of recorded incidents has increased. Police forces have created a system that allows these crimes to be identified and are encouraging individuals to report these incidents so that they can be tackled.

It is important for police managers to exhort their officers to deal with racially motivated incidents, and other such hate crimes, as a priority and to include them as such in their policing plans. It is not the job for a specialist officer, but for all officers to take on the responsibility for recording and investigating such crimes. There is often a training need for officers to implement relevant legislation and to raise their cultural awareness.

More standardisation in terms of forms and procedures are being implemented so that more accurate comparisons between forces can be made.

Crime & Disorder

The Government has made a commitment on tackling crime and the causes of crime and through their Crime and Disorder Act 1998 they place a requirement on local councils, the police and other agencies, in partnership, to conduct and publish an audit of local crime and disorder problems; consult locally on the basis of the audit; set and publish objectives and targets for the reduction of crime and disorder; monitor progress; and, repeat the process every three years.

A crime and disorder audit is required to assist partnerships establish their strategic priorities. Skilled staff who understand the policy process and are able to collate and analyse a wide variety of local data on crime and disorder, not simply the crime rates, undertake audits. Apart from police sources of data on crimes and criminals the local authorities have valuable information on the nature, distribution and costs of crime and disorder not available to the police.

The crime audit needs to provide an overview of problems - including costs where possible - to assess existing responses and to suggest provisional priorities for action. Partnership priority-setting clearly involves value judgements as well as data on problem-patterns.

Consultation is needed to check that the audit has construed problems accurately, it is comprehensive, that there are no misconceptions about communities, and to obtain opinion about priorities and options.

The crime and disorder strategy needs to be integrated with other local plans. It must be seen to bind all the relevant players together rather than a discreet policy that has no impact. The implementation of the plan may well require media involvement. This needs to be carefully thought out to prevent unrealistic expectations being created in the minds of the public.

Crime reduction work needs to be monitored to ensure that initiatives are on schedule and to ensure that modifications are made where necessary. Monitoring may also uncover future trends in crime and pre-emptive measures can be taken.

Evaluating the success of initiatives can be expensive. Often the phrase the 'light is not worth the candle' is appropriate - it is just not worth the effort. When detailed analysis is justified the police often make use of external consultants and academic institutions.

Community Safety

Tackling crime and the reducing the fear of crime cannot be achieved by the police alone. Too often organisations have 're-invented the wheel' without regard for the experience of others in the field. In future local organisations will need to work even closer together to develop comprehensive solutions that offer permanent enhancements to quality of life issues for their communities.

The Audit Commission has recognised that good practice needs to be shared and created a web site to promote case studies submitted by police and other agencies.

Preventing Vandalism

Vandalism (criminal damage) costs millions of pounds each year, can cost lives where safety is compromised and adds to the climate of fear amongst the general public.

Studies in this area have shown that publicity by itself is not enough to prevent vandalism. An educational approach designed to build up social responsibility through showing young people the consequences of vandalism may be effective.

Crime prevention measures to make targets less vulnerable through surveillance has a measurable effect, especially where the would-be culprit thinks that it can lead to immediate action, such as CCTV on public transport. There is always the possibility that vandalism may simply be displaced to softer targets elsewhere. The conspicuous presence of uniformed personnel is important in reducing vandalism. Single agency, single approach initiatives are less successful than multi-agency methods using a variety of strategies to tackle the problem.

Once the problem of vandalism has been defined by the agencies a prevention strategy is written. The counter measures could include design modifications to reduce opportunity and promote surveillance, target hardening, community initiatives and education programmes and improving management policies and practices. The best initiatives use several measures, each designed to reinforce one another. In selecting measures, it is not sufficient to base decisions solely on evidence of past success; what works in one situation may not work in another. Thought needs to be given to the effect that the measures hope to trigger, and to how far the particular context is likely to help or hinder that effect.

Implementation is managed effectively. Everyone in the partnership should know their role and be committed to co-operating in their efforts. The results of the operation should be monitored and evaluated.

With all police initiatives an 'exit strategy' is an essential. It must be made clear from the outset that with limited resources available to the police they cannot engage in an open-ended commitment to provide officers and funds for a project. At discreet intervals the operation will be assessed and sooner or later the resources will be withdrawn to be deployed to a more pressing operational need elsewhere. The question remains for the other agencies, "What will remain when the police pull out their resources?" Problems have occurred in the past where a term policing team has been deployed to a once troublesome estate, becoming in the eyes of the residents their own mini-police force. The public were disappointed when the team was withdrawn and they reverted to the normal level of police service.

Town Centre Closed Circuit Television Systems
CCTV systems can assist the police tackle crime and disorder in town centres.

Through the use of CCTV the police can deploy and manage resources more effectively.

CCTV can also be used 'patrol' areas and spot situations as they happen. Radio communication between the camera operators, the police and even local businesses are key to the success of the CCTV system in co-ordination of the response.

It is an advantage for the system to replay events in 'real-time' so that offenders can be identified. The video footage is also valuable evidence.

CCTV also has a marked impact on local crime levels. Research has shown that where town centre cameras have been installed burglaries have fallen by more than half and criminal damage was down by a third. For these benefits to continue the cameras must be seen to make arrest more likely; this requires a rapid police response. There is some anecdotal evidence to suggest that some offences of minor disorder may actually increase once a system has been installed. Before the cameras were in place many instances of minor disorder would have gone unreported, however where the camera operator spots a fight on the street officers can be expected to be deployed and arrests made.

The most successful CCTV's integrated into the command and control systems. To ensure that town centre cameras act as a deterrent the police must be seen to use them to make arrests.

Camera operators can be tasked to look for wanted or missing persons and to patrol crime hot-spots. The police need to be mindful of the displacement effect of town centre CCTV and patrol adjacent areas where there are fewer cameras more intensely.

A more recent example of town centre filming has been by special police video vans. These vans are painted in a distinctive livery and film the public at night as they go from pub to pub. Knowing that their actions will definitely be recorded seems to have a salutary effect on their behaviour.

Problem Solving and Crime Reduction

Recent research has focussed on the problem solving approaches that police forces have adopted to tackle crime.

Most crime initiatives are targeted against burglars, car thieves, drug suppliers and young offenders. It appears that in future the police will incorporate an evaluation process into their operations to provide a quantifiable measure of success.

The best operations start with a detailed analysis to define problems in a way that allows a range of options to be generated. The analysis also identifies what are called 'pinch points' which are those conditions that are necessary for the problem condition to persist. It may be vulnerable access to the rear of dwellings that could be tackled by the local authority fitting alleyway gates. This also highlights the advantage of considering a multi-agency approach from the very outset. Successful projects require detailed groundwork and consideration of the impact of interventions that the police propose rather than simply throwing resources at the problem. For the initiatives to have long-term effects the local residents need to be involved in a consultation process.

The key factors for achieving success are:
* Leaders who are committed, enthusiastic and knowledgeable.
* Problem-solving supported by practical advice and assistance.
* Sound analysis by appropriate software and professional analysts.
* Informed problem-solving backed up by information, training and experience
* Good practice circulated to others.
* Staff selection based on their abilities and aptitudes.
* Recognising problem-solving.

Forensic Science & Crime Investigation.
In the mid-1990's a project was undertaken to look at the use the police made of forensic science and the current provision of forensic science.

The study found wide variations in the numbers of Scenes of Crime Officers (SOCOs) relative to the numbers of officers or the level of crime. It also found that there was scope to enhance the quality checking of examinations and improving the knowledge amongst officers of the tests that can be done.

The current use of the national DNA database is paying dividends. There are many cases of previously undetected crimes now being solved. For example the DNA mouth swab from someone arrested for a relatively minor offence today may be matched with DNA material left at the scene of a serious undetected crime from years ago.

The fingerprint recognition database has also had similar successes. It has also given new information about the patterns of offending which have challenged conventional police wisdom. The system has found that prolific criminals do specialise in one area of activity but commit a far wider range of offences, an armed robber may also engage in petty pilfering. Matches of fingerprints have also shown that travelling criminals do not restrict their activities to the adjacent counties, but travel the length of the country on criminal escapades.

Asset Stripping the Proceeds of Crime

In the past the amounts of money made by criminals, especially premier league drug suppliers, have been 'modest'.

UK research has estimated that the amount available for profit confiscation from criminals is more than £500 million (excluding fraud offences) each year. In 1993 confiscation orders totalled only £14 million.

There are many reasons why so little of the assets are recovered. Despite all of the problems the police should always consider freezing and stripping the proceeds of crime from criminals.

This calls for financial investigation trained officers to assist inquiries and co-ordinate efforts of prosecutors and financiers to trace, identify, freeze and seize assets. There could be an added incentive for the police service, or even specific investigation units, if they could retain a percentage of the seizures.

Government plans have included making inmates pay for their keep whilst in prison. The money would come from their financial assets. Many criminals however lead chaotic lifestyles and have no financial resources.

Intelligence, Surveillance & Informants

It is widely accepted that intelligence-led policing is more effective than simple reactive policing. Intelligence-led policing relies on quality information from surveillance and informants.

To make a real difference in operational terms the structure and culture of the organisation needs to be intelligence-driven. Simply taking individual proactive measures such as surveillance teams, registered informants and an intelligence system, seem only to make a marginal impact on crime.

For intelligence-led policing to be effective requires the wholehearted commitment from all concerned from senior officers through to officers on the front-line. To that end a clear strategy is needed so that all officers involved understand the interdependence of the roles in the proactive system so that they can make an effective contribution.

Progress needs to be monitored and successes shared with all the officers.

The Future of Patrol

Privately paid security officers have been a feature of policing in Britain for centuries. The positive role of night watchmen and others who protect property has long been accepted by the police. The problems emerge when private people 'police' other people in shopping centres, on housing estates and in pubs and clubs. Issues such as the selection, training and accountability of these private individuals are a concern.

There are two courses of action open to the police, refuse to interact in any way with the private companies or co-operate with them. These companies are often keen to be officially recognised by the police and to screen criminals from applying for security jobs. Forces could benefit by having additional uniformed presence on the streets.

This is a debate that has yet to be resolved.

Patten Commission Report

As part of the Good Friday agreement the ex-Governor of Hong Kong and Conservative minister Chris Patten led a commission into the future of policing in Northern Ireland.

The RUC G.C. has, in 2001, become the Northern Ireland Police Service (PSNI). It has borne the brunt of tackling Terrorism in the province since the start of the most recent troubles for more than three decades has claimed the lives of more than three hundred officers and nearly ten thousand injured in addition to the tragic deaths of thousands of members of the armed forces and civilians from both traditions. The impact of policing a troubled society not only affects the physical survival of the officer, but also his or her family. Many police families have had to move home in fear of intimidation. Some Catholic officers have been ostracised by their families.

Opinion of the RUC, now the PSNI, is sometimes divided between those who believe that it represents the interests of the Protestant community and those that see it as the bulwark against terrorism. The Patten Commission was set up to recommend measures to make the police service in Northern Ireland more acceptable to the majority of the public. With the importance placed on symbolism by each tradition it was clear that some suggestions regarding the badge, name and flying the flag of union would attract controversy. For those officers and their loved ones who have paid the ultimate price for serving a community the change of name and cap badge is an emotive issue. Those officers wore the badge with pride, change will be painful. The proposals for a new oath of allegiance without reference to the Sovereign could make joining the police more palatable for recruits from some sections of the community, but may cause insult to others. The new oath contains references to upholding human rights.

The Patten Commission is attempting to weaken the link between the Central Government through the Northern Ireland office and the PSNI by making the police more accountable to local stakeholders as it is in the rest of the UK. These local arrangements will include a police board and a police ombudsman.

With most of the major para-military organisations on ceasefire a downsizing of the PSNI is being contemplated. If the security situation stabilises a future police service in Northern Ireland may be smaller; wholly full-time; and with a greater proportion of Catholics. The reduction in strength would be achieved through financial severance packages for serving officers and reservists. The recruitment would be through an independent civilian organisation to provide the police service with future officers 50: 50 ratios of Protestants and Catholics. This would need legislative change, as it would contravene existing anti-discrimination employment law. The peace dividend savings will include less reliance on firearms training and the provision of protected vehicles.

If all the changes are going to bring about a genuine renaissance in community relationships then the gain may be worth the pain that the Commission's report will mean. The future of the troubled province requires a genuine commitment and courage from para-military leaders to resolve difficulties within the law and consign their arsenals of weapons and explosives to the past.

Technology
With cyber-crime increasing, e.g., pornography, fraud and terrorism, police boundaries are less relevant. Legislation needs to catch up with latest means of criminals exploiting the information technology.

The police can and are making use of technology to respond to demand. Computers have improved command and control systems. They are even making an impact on the streets with officers shortly to be equipped with new Airwave (formerly PSRCP and PSRCS) personal communication devices offering a host of facilities. Mobile data terminals will also make a significant difference to the service delivered by frontline officers. GPS devices will be able to pinpoint officers' locations as an aid to their safety and effective deployment.

The future of vehicle law enforcement will depend on advances in technology, possibly limiting the speed vehicles can achieve on certain stretches of road. Facial recognition software, linked to CCTV and a database could improve the detection of wanted and missing persons. Automatic number plate devices have already proved successful in combating car crime.

Every technological advance will need to be compliant with the liberties of individuals balanced against the protection of society as a whole.

Devolved Budgets
It is often seen as good practice for local BCU commanders to be given control over their own budgets. The commanders then become responsible for achieving effective and efficient use of their available resources.

Commanders joined the service to be police officers, not accountants and to ensure proper control over their operational initiatives they will use project management methods more and more.

Frameworks based on simple project management principles assist commanders to run initiatives from simple ones to large-scale multi-agency operations involving significant resources.

Project Management

Increasingly strategic decisions such as the introduction of new communication systems and capital building projects like a new headquarters will be based on project methodology. One methodology is PRINCE (Project Management in Controlled Environments). This government owned methodology is widely used in the police and public service. It ensures that projects are properly run and involve the suppliers and the users throughout the process. Each step and decision is documented and approval is necessary before a project board under takes the next stage. This reduces the risk involved in large projects that safeguard public money.

Calling the Police

As the majority of public-police interaction is by telephone switchboards, call handlers and control rooms are crucial. This first point of contact influences the perception of the public about their police service - the police have only one chance to make their first impression. It needs to be right.

Control rooms represent at least five per cent of expenditure. For the provincial forces of England and Wales that translates to about £ 160 m each year. They handle about 40 million calls including at least 12 million emergency calls. They deploy 65,000 officers to 17 million incidents, six million of which need an immediate response.

Communication deliver a quality service by answering calls quickly; obtaining accurate information swiftly and politely; reassuring callers and giving advice in stressful situations; grading the police response; providing unambiguous directions to operational officers.

Performance is monitored to measure, amongst other things, the time taken to answer calls and how quickly officers attend incidents.

Deploying officers appropriately is an important area as resources are expensive. It has been estimated that is costs £300,000 a year to pay for a double-crewed vehicle available 24 hours a day.

Research has shown that cost of communications centres varies between police forces - from £1260 per police officer each year in one force to nearly £2160 in another.

Financial savings of approximately 15 per cent could be made in control rooms by greater efficiency and civilianisation. This equates to about £25m annually.

In future control rooms are likely to be amalgamated into ever-larger units to gain economy of scale. Operators will work a flexible shift pattern to match resources with demand rather than a traditional four-shift system. Civilians will replace police officers as control room operators. New technology in the form of help desk software will assist call handlers to offer expert advice. Increasingly there will be one-tier control rooms rather than a hierarchy with a central control room and satellites serving divisions or BCUs.

Recruitment and Retention
The police are currently facing important internal issues especially with the recruitment and retention of officers. Due partly to the buoyant economy the police starting salary is less attractive than it has been in the past. This has been exacerbated by the fact that since 1994 new entrants have not been eligible for money to subsidise their housing costs. As a result Forces with a high cost of living have experienced difficulty in retaining officers. To stem the tide of officers transferring to other Forces the Metropolitan Police have provided an enhanced financial package for some of their officers. This has had a knock-on effect for Forces in the Home Counties who have been considering ways to retain their officers. The situation has yet to be resolved and there may be a possibility of some form of regional pay being arrived at.

In the constant change in policing. the only thing you can predict is that the future will, thankfully, be unpredictable. Police have to face ever increasing (and often contradictory) demands on their limited resources.

CHAPTER 6. POLICE TRAINING

Due to its unpredictable nature police work can be extremely demanding. This calls for people with a wide range of knowledge, understanding, skills, abilities and behaviour.

Almost every time that new laws are passed the police need to train its staff to be able to implement the legislation. Due to developments in policing more training is required to tackle emerging trends, such as high technology crime. As with other institutions, heightened awareness of community and race relations has become necessary for the police in the wake of the Macpherson Report.

One of the main concepts is training for reality. The training that officers receive is directly linked to improving their on-the-job performance. The bedrock of police training is their foundation course.

Foundation Course

Although once called 'basic training', the Foundation Course develops a recruit into a competent officer, who can safely and effectively fulfil the 'office of constable'. In other words they are fit to operate independently and deal with whatever job they encounter.

Whether the recruit has previous relevant experience as a cadet, has served in the police branches of the armed forces, or is a complete newcomer, the training is exactly the same.

The recruits spend the first week or two at their own police force on an induction course before they go to the regional National Police Training (NPT) Centre for a 15-week course. While they are at their 'home' force they are issued with their uniform, get to know about their Force and are sworn in front of a local magistrate. From that moment onwards they are 'constables' with all the powers and responsibility that goes with it. (In the Metropolitan Police Service this 'swearing in' is done in front of a senior officer.)

At the NPT Centre officers will work alongside colleagues from neighbouring police forces and will progress through an intensive programme. Although the Metropolitan Police has its own centre at Hendon other forces use centres based around the regions;
Ashford (South East),
Bruche (North West),
Cwmbran (South Wales),
Durham (North East),
Ryton (Midlands),
Tulliallan (Scotland),
Brooklyn (Northern Ireland).

Sometimes other sites are used. The training is both mentally and physically demanding.

The legislation and procedural aspects are covered in classroom-based activities and are reinforced by practical scenarios. Officers' confidence grows as the training progresses and they address their concerns and expectations about their chosen career. Feedback is given to the officers throughout their foundation course so that they know how they are developing. The officers have to take written examinations to test their knowledge and go through practical situations to show how they can apply their newly learnt skills. These scenarios can be based in simulated shops, pubs and houses.

The varied programme also includes fitness training, first aid, swimming, self-defence and public order. Although the tempo of the course is brisk there is also some time to unwind and socialise. Though most officers stay at the centre during the week others return home, especially if they have domestic commitments. After passing out from their NPT Centre the officers return to their own Force for a short course on local procedures before moving on to their police station for their first shift.

Officers turning up for duty for their first time are understandably excited at the prospect of going 'operational' and yet have concerns as to how they are going to deal with the unknown. First of all they are introduced to an experienced officer - their tutor constable. Their tutors will accompany them for the next ten weeks gradually allowing them to do more and more work as their effectiveness increases. At the end of this period a decision is made to allow officers to go it alone and their report is marked up, 'Fit for independent patrol.'

From this point on the officers can work on their own, but still return to their local training centre for a few weeks of modular training during the remainder of their two year probationary period. These additional courses will assist the officers to hone their skills and help them improve their performance.

Providing that their work has been acceptable officers pass their probationary period and they receive notification that their 'appointment has been confirmed'.

Once the two-year probationary period has been completed officers may wish to consolidate their local knowledge, foster community links and remain serving their area as a uniformed officer. They can also develop their police skills further by joining a specialist department, for example the CID or Traffic, or going for the promotion process. Specialisation and promotion require personal development and there are associated training courses available.

Specialist Training

CID

After working through a distance-learning package, apprentice detectives undertake a course, which deepens their knowledge of the criminal law. The training also includes how to deal with serious crimes, from preserving forensic evidence at the scene, through the investigative process to interviewing witnesses and suspects.

Specialist officers also get trained in surveillance (and anti-surveillance) techniques. There are also courses for technical surveillance where, with appropriate authorisation, the unlawful activities of top criminals can be monitored.

UNIFORM OPERATIONS

Traffic

Traffic training includes driving courses that take standard drivers through to being the safest drivers on the roads today - the advanced driver.

Traffic patrol officers are introduced to intricate areas of traffic law, such as that relating to heavy goods vehicles, drivers' hours and tachographs. Their knowledge of ensuring the safety of the travelling public through a process of education, road engineering and law enforcement is enhanced.

Accident investigation is a complex area of police work requiring the skills of detective with the ability to apply mathematical formulae to reconstruct serious road traffic collisions.

Public Order

Certain officers are given advanced training in dealing with outbreaks of disorder. This takes an officer through from basic crowd control techniques through to facing an all-out riot with bricks, bottles and petrol bombs being thrown.

Additional training is given to other officers who have to take command of these incidents. These commanders, assisted by trained advisors, can resolve critical incidents be they a large group of rioters through to a single barricaded individual.

Firearms

Officers usually volunteer for firearms duty. After a rigorous application process candidates undergo weeks of training to develop their abilities in the law, decision-making, tactics and weapon handling.

Once qualified the firearms officers can be deployed as a member of an Armed Response Vehicle crew or can be called out to form part of a firearms team to deal with a pre-planned operation. Throughout the year officers have to re-qualify both on the range and pass a physical test and medical in addition to receiving regular tactical training sessions.

Custody Officer Training

Through a process of distance learning and classroom training Sergeants are prepared for the demanding role of custody officer. A custody officer is responsible for the cellblock at a local police station and for ensuring that the rights of people who have been arrested are respected.

MANAGEMENT TRAINING

Sergeant and Inspector Training

On promotion to Sergeant and Inspector officers attend training to improve their supervisory and managerial skills. They need to be able to manage people who work for them and to deal with tasks such as business plans and police operations.

Strategic Training

Additional training is given to senior officers at command level to give them a strategic perspective. These courses are demanding and are held at the police staff college, Bramshill.

The number and type of police training courses is immense, reflecting the diverse nature of police work. Many are to a national standard and are held only at certain police training colleges that may have specific facilities, such as the several national firearms training centres, who are NPT accredited, having, for example, suitable range facilities. Other courses are devised locally to suit the needs of individual forces, usually carried out after a 'training needs analysis'.

CHAPTER 7. NATIONAL OVERVIEW

Statistics are for the Home Office, Scottish Office or Northern Ireland Office police forces of England, Wales, Scotland and Northern Ireland unless stated otherwise.

Population of Force Areas   59,386,582

Ethnic Minority Population (excluding Northern Ireland)   3,218,821

Size of Force Areas   151,283 km²

Financial Resources		
Financial Year	1998-1999	1999-2000
Expenditure (£ Million)	9,413	8,829
Cost per resident per day	43.4 p	40.7 p

Human Resources			
Financial Year		1998-1999	1999-2000
Regular Police Officers	ACPO	235	233
	Superintendent	1,570	1,572
	Chief Inspector	1,990	1,941
	Inspector	7,185	7,157
	Sergeant	22,151	21,876
	Constable	113,959	112,378
	Total Regular Police Officers	147,720	145,157
	Superintendent Female Officers to Residents	1:402	1:409
Auxiliary Police Officers[1]		22,205	19,694
	Total	60,691	60,105
	National number of support staff per 100 regular police officers	41.09	41.41

---

[1] Special Constables and PSNI Reservists
[2] Excluding Northern Ireland

Health Issues		
Financial year	1998-1999	1999-2000
Average annual sick days - Regular Police Officers (excluding Scotland and Northern Ireland)	11.68	11.55
Average annual sick days - Civilian Support Staff (excluding Scotland and Northern Ireland)	12.34	12.35
Number of assaults on police officers (excluding Scotland and Northern Ireland)	12,533	11,461
Number of sickness days lost as a result of assault (excluding Northern Ireland)	35,062	23,370
Police working days lost through sickness (excluding Northern Ireland)	1,596,188	1,556,519

PERFORMANCE		
	1998-1999	1999-2000
Number of emergency calls (excluding Scotland and Northern Ireland)	7,990,070	9,315,002
Calls for service (excluding Scotland and Northern Ireland)	17,801,151	18,442,588
Number of recorded complaints	36,365	37,049
Number of substantiated complaints	1,307	1,131
Crime Performance		
Recorded crimes	5,652,093	5,855,913
Crimes per 10,000 population	952	986
Detected crimes	1,714,811	1,560,192
Number of crimes detected per officer per year	11.6	10.7
Number of arrests (excluding Scotland and Northern Ireland)	1,348,918	1,237,538
Number of racial incidents (excluding Scotland and Northern Ireland)	24,320	49,870
Stop and search - White (excluding Scotland and Northern Ireland)	870,603	697,565
Stop and search - Ethnic Minority (excluding Scotland and Northern Ireland)	156,835	112,035
Road Traffic Collisions		
Fatal RTC	3,525	3,548
Serious Injury RTC	41,546	40,153
Other RTC	287,493	285,029
Total Injury RTCs	332,564	328,730

CHAPTER 8. POLICE FORCES

This Chapter gives basic details of each of the fifty-two geographic forces of the United Kingdom in alphabetical order.

The postal address, telephone numbers and website address of each force is listed.

The names of the Chief Constables are listed.

Also to be found are statistics covering the size of the force areas, emergency calls answered, and crime and road collisions figures.

AVON & SOMERSET CONSTABULARY

PO Box 37, Portishead, Bristol BS20 8QJ
Telephone: 01275 818181
Website: www.avsom.police.uk

Chief Constable; S.C. Pilkington, Esq., Q.P.M.

Force General Statistics

Population of Force Area	1,488,700
Size of Force Area km²	4,804 km²
Annual expenditure (£ million)	169.9
Cost per resident per day	31p

Force divisions and staff

Number of territorial divisions	8
Total number of officers	2,934
Total number of Specials	459
Total number of civilian support staff	1,495

Calls from the public

Number of emergency calls	242,832
Calls for service	420,521

Crime

Recorded crimes	147,104
Crimes per 10,000 population	988
Detected crimes	32,041

Road Traffic Collisions

Fatal RTCs	75
Total Injury RTCs	7,509

Health

Police days lost through sickness	34,485
Number of assaults on police	405

BEDFORDSHIRE POLICE

Woburn Road, Kempston, Bedford, MK43 9AX
Telephone 01234 841212
Website www.bedfordshire.police.uk

Chief Constable; Mr M. O'Byrne Q.P.M. L.L.B.

Force General Statistics

Population of Force Area	556,628
Size of Force Area km^2	1,235 km^2
Annual expenditure (£ million)	63,307
Cost per resident per day	31p

Force divisions and staff

Number of territorial divisions	3
Total number of officers	1,027
Total number of Specials	151
Total number of civilian support staff	498

Calls from the public

Number of emergency calls	74,464
Calls for service	143,140

Crime

Recorded crimes	53,607
Crimes per 10,000 population	963
Detected crimes	13,313

Road Traffic Collisions

Fatal RTCs	79
Total Injury RTCs	2,836

Health

Police days lost through sickness	12,853
Number of assaults on police	97

CAMBRIDGESHIRE CONSTABULARY

Hinchingbrooke Park, Huntingdon, PE29 6NP
Telephone 01480 456111
Website www.cambs.police.uk

Chief Constable; Mr D.G. Gunn, Q.P.M. M.A.(Cantab)

Force General Statistics

Population of Force Area	719,800
Size of Force Area km²	3,409
Annual expenditure (£ million)	74.38
Cost per resident per day	28p

Force divisions and staff

Number of territorial divisions	3
Total number of officers	1,027
Total number of Specials	274
Total number of civilian support staff	498

Calls from the public

Number of emergency calls	104,306
Calls for service	209,337

Crime

Recorded crimes	68,722
Crimes per 10,000 population	955
Detected crimes	17,395

Road Traffic Collisions

Fatal RTCs	76
Total Injury RTCs	4,393

Health

Police days lost through sickness	15,003
Number of assaults on police	160

CENTRAL SCOTLAND POLICE

Police Headquarters, Randolphfield, Stirling, FK8 2HD
Telephone 01786 456000
Website www.scottish.police.uk

Chief Constable; Mr W.J.M. Wilson, Q.P.M.

Force General Statistics

Population of Force Area	277,600
Size of Force Area km²	2,632
Annual expenditure (£ million)	34.37
Cost per resident per day	34p

Force divisions and staff

Number of territorial divisions	3
Total number of officers	721
Total number of Specials	60
Total number of civilian support staff	206

Calls from the public

Number of emergency calls	N/k
Calls for service	N/k

Crime

Recorded crimes	17,336
Crimes per 10,000 population	624
Detected crimes	9,535

Road Traffic Collisions

Fatal RTCs	9
Total Injury RTCs	735

Health

Police days lost through sickness	8,673
Number of assaults on police	N/k

CHESHIRE CONSTABULARY

Castle Esplanade, Chester, CH1 2PP
Telephone 01244 350000
Website www.cheshire.police.uk

Chief Constable; Mr N.K. Burgess, Q.P.M., B.A.

Force General Statistics

Population of Force Area	984,280
Size of Force Area km²	2,333
Annual expenditure (£ million)	1110.66
Cost per resident per day	31p

Force divisions and staff

Number of territorial divisions	6
Total number of officers	2,010
Total number of Specials	350
Total number of civilian support staff	848

Calls from the public

Number of emergency calls	134,361
Calls for service	292,425

Crime

Recorded crimes	64,528
Crimes per 10,000 population	656
Detected crimes	19,884

Road Traffic Collisions

Fatal RTCs	75
Total Injury RTCs	9,939

Health

Police days lost through sickness	25,027
Number of assaults on police	239

CITY OF LONDON POLICE

26, Old Jewry, London, EC2R 8DJ
Telephone 020 7601 2222
Website www.cityoflondon.police.uk

Commissioner; Mr P. Nove, Q.P.M.

Force General Statistics

Population of Force Area	303,000*
Size of Force Area km²	3
Annual expenditure (£ million)	57.22
Cost per resident per day	52p*

Force divisions and staff

Number of territorial divisions	2
Total number of officers	735
Total number of Specials	55
Total number of civilian support staff	284

Calls from the public

Number of emergency calls	N/a*
Calls for service	35,439

Crime

Recorded crimes	7,775
Crimes per 10,000 population	257
Detected crimes	2,498

Road Traffic Collisions

Fatal RTCs	1
Total Injury RTCs	509

Health

Police days lost through sickness	9,571
Number of assaults on police	44

1. * Population are almost solely workers, travelling in and out each day.
.2. Emergency calls are routed to the Metropolitan police.

CLEVELAND POLICE

PO Box 70, Ladgate Lane, Middlesbrough, TS8 9EH
Telephone 01642 326326
Website www.cleveland.police.uk

Chief Constable; Mr B. Shaw, Q.P.M., B.A.(Hons)

Force General Statistics

Population of Force Area	556,300
Size of Force Area km^2	590
Annual expenditure (£ million)	82.77
Cost per resident per day	41p

Force divisions and staff

Number of territorial divisions	4
Total number of officers	1420
Total number of Specials	128
Total number of civilian support staff	596

Calls from the public

Number of emergency calls	99,665
Calls for service	224,720

Crime

Recorded crimes	7,775
Crimes per 10,000 population	257
Detected crimes	2,498

Road Traffic Collisions

Fatal RTCs	1
Total Injury RTCs	509

Health

Police days lost through sickness	9,571
Number of assaults on police	44

CUMBRIA CONSTABULARY

Carleton Hall, Penrith, Cumbria, CA10 2AU
Telephone 01768 891999
Website www.cumbria.police.uk

Chief Constable; Mr C. Phillips Q.P.M.

Force General Statistics

Population of Force Area	492,884
Size of Force Area km²	6,810
Annual expenditure (£ million)	65.16
Cost per resident per day	36p

Force divisions and staff

Number of territorial divisions	3
Total number of officers	1,083
Total number of Specials	176
Total number of civilian support staff	475

Calls from the public

Number of emergency calls	47,516
Calls for service	211,234

Crime

Recorded crimes	37,729
Crimes per 10,000 population	765
Detected crimes	14,830

Road Traffic Collisions

Fatal RTCs	62
Total Injury RTCs	2,990

Health

Police days lost through sickness	13,286
Number of assaults on police	103

DERBYSHIRE CONSTABULARY

Butterley Hall, Ripley, Derbyshire DE5 3RS
Telephone 01773 570100
Website www.derbyshire.police.uk

Chief Constable; Mr J.F. Newing C.B.E., Q.P.M., B.A.(Hons)

Force General Statistics

Population of Force Area	974,000
Size of Force Area km²	2,629
Annual expenditure (£ million)	105.39
Cost per resident per day	30p

Force divisions and staff

Number of territorial divisions	4
Total number of officers	1,776
Total number of Specials	283
Total number of civilian support staff	897

Calls from the public

Number of emergency calls	126,060
Calls for service	268,122

Crime

Recorded crimes	85,650
Crimes per 10,000 population	879
Detected crimes	23,846

Road Traffic Collisions

Fatal RTCs	60
Total Injury RTCs	5,519

Health

Police days lost through sickness	22,156
Number of assaults on police	278

DEVON AND CORNWALL CONSTABULARY

Middlemoor, Exeter, EX2 7HQ
Telephone 0990 777444
Website www.devon-cornwall.police.uk

Chief Constable; Sir John Evans, Q.P.M., LL.B.

Force General Statistics

Population of Force Area	1,567,000
Size of Force Area km²	10,241
Annual expenditure (£ million)	175.22
Cost per resident per day	31p

Force divisions and staff

Number of territorial divisions	4 (areas)
Total number of officers	2,840
Total number of Specials	870
Total number of civilian support staff	1,462

Calls from the public

Number of emergency calls	206,823
Calls for service	467,009

Crime

Recorded crimes	110,361
Crimes per 10,000 population	704
Detected crimes	38,743

Road Traffic Collisions

Fatal RTCs	78
Total Injury RTCs	7,647

Health

Police days lost through sickness	31,549
Number of assaults on police	311

DORSET POLICE

Winfrith, Dorchester, Dorset, DT2 8DZ
Telephone 01929 462727
Website www.dorset.police.uk

Chief Constable; Mrs J. Stichbury, B.A. M.A.

Force General Statistics

Population of Force Area	691,710
Size of Force Area km²	2,653
Annual expenditure (£ million)	76.06
Cost per resident per day	30p

Force divisions and staff

Number of territorial divisions	4
Total number of officers	1,305
Total number of Specials	298
Total number of civilian support staff	686

Calls from the public

Number of emergency calls	79,772
Calls for service	159,373

Crime

Recorded crimes	52,332
Crimes per 10,000 population	757
Detected crimes	13,488

Road Traffic Collisions

Fatal RTCs	35
Total Injury RTCs	3,835

Health

Police days lost through sickness	13,224
Number of assaults on police	168

DUMFRIES AND GALLOWAY CONSTABULARY

Cornwall Mount, Dumfries, DG1 1PZ
Telephone 01387 252112
Website www.scottish.police.uk

Chief Constable; Mr W. Rae, Q.P.M.

Force General Statistics

Population of Force Area	146,800
Size of Force Area km²	6,370
Annual expenditure (£ million)	22.03
Cost per resident per day	41p

Force divisions and staff

Number of territorial divisions	2
Total number of officers	451
Total number of Specials	163
Total number of civilian support staff	208

Calls from the public

Number of emergency calls	N/k
Calls for service	N/k

Crime

Recorded crimes	8,269
Crimes per 10,000 population	563
Detected crimes	4,631

Road Traffic Collisions

Fatal RTCs	12
Total Injury RTCs	388

Health

Police days lost through sickness	3,413
Number of assaults on police	N/k

DURHAM CONSTABULARY

Aykley Heads, Durham, DH1 5TT
Telephone 0191 386 4929
Website www.durham.police.uk

Chief Constable; Mr G.E. Hedges, Q.P.M.

Force General Statistics

Population of Force Area	607,770
Size of Force Area km²	2,434
Annual expenditure (£ million)	80.56
Cost per resident per day	36p

Force divisions and staff

Number of territorial divisions	6
Total number of officers	1,557
Total number of Specials	157
Total number of civilian support staff	643

Calls from the public

Number of emergency calls	61,657
Calls for service	198,427

Crime

Recorded crimes	48,796
Crimes per 10,000 population	803
Detected crimes	15,713

Road Traffic Collisions

Fatal RTCs	33
Total Injury RTCs	2,646

Health

Police days lost through sickness	16,795
Number of assaults on police	221

DYFED-POWYS POLICE

PO Box 99, Llangunnor, Carmarthen, SA31 2PF
Telephone 01267 222020
Website www.dyfed-powys.police.uk

Chief Constable; Mr R. White, C.B.E. Q.P.M. C.I.Mgt

Force General Statistics

Population of Force Area	474,700
Size of Force Area km²	10,944
Annual expenditure (£ million)	55.71
Cost per resident per day	32p

Force divisions and staff

Number of territorial divisions	6
Total number of officers	1,040
Total number of Specials	202
Total number of civilian support staff	389

Calls from the public

Number of emergency calls	39,689
Calls for service	128,433

Crime

Recorded crimes	23,709
Crimes per 10,000 population	499
Detected crimes	15,411

Road Traffic Collisions

Fatal RTCs	48
Total Injury RTCs	2,487

Health

Police days lost through sickness	11,493
Number of assaults on police	89

ESSEX POLICE

PO Box 2, Springfield, Chelmsford, Essex, CM2 6DA
Telephone 01245 491491
Website www.essex.police.uk

Chief Constable; Mr D.F. Stevens, Q.P.M. LL.B.

Force General Statistics

Population of Force Area	1,533,255
Size of Force Area km²	3,594
Annual expenditure (£ million)	169.68
Cost per resident per day	30p

Force divisions and staff

Number of territorial divisions	10
Total number of officers	2,805
Total number of Specials	483
Total number of civilian support staff	1,450

Calls from the public

Number of emergency calls	206,635
Calls for service	390,545

Crime

Recorded crimes	102,777
Crimes per 10,000 population	670
Detected crimes	30,503

Road Traffic Collisions

Fatal RTCs	106
Total Injury RTCs	8,691

Health

Police days lost through sickness	40,919
Number of assaults on police	170

FIFE CONSTABULARY

Detroit Road, Glenrothes, Fife, KY6 2RJ
Telephone 01592 418888
Website www.scottish.police.uk

Chief Constable; Mr J.P. Hamilton, Q.P.M. B.A.(Hons) M.B.A. B.Sc.

Force General Statistics

Population of Force Area	349,200
Size of Force Area km²	1,307
Annual expenditure (£ million)	43.28
Cost per resident per day	34p

Force divisions and staff

Number of territorial divisions	3
Total number of officers	838
Total number of Specials	97
Total number of civilian support staff	285

Calls from the public

Number of emergency calls	N/k
Calls for service	N/k

Crime

Recorded crimes	27,601
Crimes per 10,000 population	790
Detected crimes	11,868

Road Traffic Collisions

Fatal RTCs	14
Total Injury RTCs	710

Health

Police days lost through sickness	8,818
Number of assaults on police	N/k

GLOUCESTERSHIRE CONSTABULARY

Holland House, Lansdown Road, Cheltenham, Gloucestershire, GL51 6 QH
Telephone 01242 521321
Website www.gloucestershire.police.uk

Chief Constable; Mr A.J.P. Butler, C.B.E. Q.P.M. B.Soc.Sc. Ph.D. C.Pyscol. A.F.B.Ps.S.

Force General Statistics

Population of Force Area	557,274
Size of Force Area km^2	2,655
Annual expenditure (£ million)	66.19
Cost per resident per day	33p

Force divisions and staff

Number of territorial divisions	3
Total number of officers	1,113
Total number of Specials	233
Total number of civilian support staff	516

Calls from the public

Number of emergency calls	67,994
Calls for service	221,348

Crime

Recorded crimes	50,993
Crimes per 10,000 population	915
Detected crimes	15,552

Road Traffic Collisions

Fatal RTCs	47
Total Injury RTCs	2,796

Health

Police days lost through sickness	11,433
Number of assaults on police	143

GRAMPIAN POLICE

Queen Street, Aberdeen, AB10 1ZA
Telephone 01224 386000
Website www.scottish.police.uk

Chief Constable; Mr A.G. Brown, Q.P.M.

Force General Statistics

Population of Force Area	525,300
Size of Force Area km²	8,704
Annual expenditure (£ million)	68.35
Cost per resident per day	36p

Force divisions and staff

Number of territorial divisions	5
Total number of officers	1,216
Total number of Specials	120
Total number of civilian support staff	508

Calls from the public

Number of emergency calls	N/k
Calls for service	N/k

Crime

Recorded crimes	48,262
Crimes per 10,000 population	919
Detected crimes	17,374

Road Traffic Collisions

Fatal RTCs	35
Total Injury RTCs	1,239

Health

Police days lost through sickness	7,522
Number of assaults on police	N/k

GREATER MANCHESTER POLICE

PO Box 22, Chester House, Boyer Street, Manchester, M16 0RE
Telephone 0161 872 5050
Website www.gmp.police.uk

Chief Constable; Mr D. Wilmot, Q.P.M. D.L.B.Sc.

Force General Statistics

Population of Force Area	2,577,434
Size of Force Area km^2	1,282
Annual expenditure (£ million)	378.73
Cost per resident per day	40p

Force divisions and staff

Number of territorial divisions	11
Total number of officers	6,794
Total number of Specials	457
Total number of civilian support staff	2,873

Calls from the public

Number of emergency calls	578,719
Calls for service	1,213,595

Crime

Recorded crimes	377,086
Crimes per 10,000 population	1,463
Detected crimes	88,470

Road Traffic Collisions

Fatal RTCs	89
Total Injury RTCs	16,488

Health

Police days lost through sickness	95,359
Number of assaults on police	941

GWENT CONSTABULARY

Croesyceiliog, Cwmbran, Torfaen, NP44 2XJ
Telephone 01633 838111
Website www.gwent.police.uk

Chief Constable; Mr K. Turner.

Force General Statistics

Population of Force Area	557,227
Size of Force Area km^2	1,556
Annual expenditure (£ million)	71.17
Cost per resident per day	35p

Force divisions and staff

Number of territorial divisions	4
Total number of officers	1,263
Total number of Specials	119
Total number of civilian support staff	527

Calls from the public

Number of emergency calls	73,226
Calls for service	205,696

Crime

Recorded crimes	60,132
Crimes per 10,000 population	1,079
Detected crimes	31,755

Road Traffic Collisions

Fatal RTCs	30
Total Injury RTCs	2,570

Health

Police days lost through sickness	16,872
Number of assaults on police	205

HAMPSHIRE CONSTABULARY

West hill, Winchester, Hants, SO22 5DB
Telephone 0845 045 45 45
Website www.hampshire.police.uk

Chief Constable; Mr P.R. Kernaghan, Q.P.M. LL.B.

Force General Statistics

Population of Force Area	1,762,500
Size of Force Area km²	4,161
Annual expenditure (£ million)	196.78
Cost per resident per day	31p

Force divisions and staff

Number of territorial divisions	11
Total number of officers	3,418
Total number of Specials	615
Total number of civilian support staff	1,496

Calls from the public

Number of emergency calls	269,027
Calls for service	540,997

Crime

Recorded crimes	135,174
Crimes per 10,000 population	767
Detected crimes	42,935

Road Traffic Collisions

Fatal RTCs	100
Total Injury RTCs	9,490

Health

Police days lost through sickness	35,518
Number of assaults on police	385

HERTFORDSHIRE CONSTABULARY

Stanborough Road, Welwyn Garden City, Herts, AL8 6XF
Telephone 01707 354200
Website www.herts.police.uk

Chief Constable; Mr P. Acres, Q.P.M.

Force General Statistics

Population of Force Area	880,779
Size of Force Area km²	1,487
Annual expenditure (£ million)	103.69
Cost per resident per day	32p

Force divisions and staff

Number of territorial divisions	9
Total number of officers	1,767
Total number of Specials	216
Total number of civilian support staff	928

Calls from the public

Number of emergency calls	132,878
Calls for service	346,326

Crime

Recorded crimes	52,741
Crimes per 10,000 population	599
Detected crimes	14,155

Road Traffic Collisions

Fatal RTCs	47
Total Injury RTCs	5,714

Health

Police days lost through sickness	18,432
Number of assaults on police	160

HUMBERSIDE POLICE

Queens Gardens, Kingston upon Hull, Humberside, HU1 3DJ
Telephone 01482 326111
Website www.humberside.police.uk

Chief Constable; Mr D. Westwood, M.A.(Oxon), Ph.D.

Force General Statistics

Population of Force Area	883,100
Size of Force Area km²	3,508
Annual expenditure (£ million)	113,131
Cost per resident per day	35p

Force divisions and staff

Number of territorial divisions	4
Total number of officers	1,882
Total number of Specials	246
Total number of civilian support staff	841

Calls from the public

Number of emergency calls	117,289
Calls for service	398,088

Crime

Recorded crimes	121,422
Crimes per 10,000 population	1,375
Detected crimes	22,534

Road Traffic Collisions

Fatal RTCs	76
Total Injury RTCs	4,510

Health

Police days lost through sickness	18,104
Number of assaults on police	265

KENT COUNTY CONSTABULARY

Sutton Road, Maidstone, Kent, ME15 9BZ
Telephone 01622 690690
Website www.kent.police.uk

Chief Constable; Mr J.D. Phillips, Q.P.M. B.A.(Econ)

Force General Statistics

Population of Force Area	1,574,561
Size of Force Area km²	3,732
Annual expenditure (£ million)	182.42
Cost per resident per day	32p

Force divisions and staff

Number of territorial divisions	9
Total number of officers	3,203
Total number of Specials	436
Total number of civilian support staff	1,648

Calls from the public

Number of emergency calls	209,215
Calls for service	426,850

Crime

Recorded crimes	124,918
Crimes per 10,000 population	793
Detected crimes	41,015

Road Traffic Collisions

Fatal RTCs	100
Total Injury RTCs	8,023

Health

Police days lost through sickness	34,681
Number of assaults on police	292

LANCASHIRE CONSTABULARY

PO Box 77, Hutton, Preston, Lancs, PR4 5SB
Telephone 01772 614444
Website www.lancs.police.uk

Chief Constable; Mrs P. Clare, Q.P.M. D.L. B.A.(Hons), C.I.Mgt.

Force General Statistics

Population of Force Area	1,426,839
Size of Force Area km^2	3,055
Annual expenditure (£ million)	177.99
Cost per resident per day	34p

Force divisions and staff

Number of territorial divisions	6
Total number of officers	3,220
Total number of Specials	382
Total number of civilian support staff	1,392

Calls from the public

Number of emergency calls	199,547
Calls for service	660,476

Crime

Recorded crimes	108,866
Crimes per 10,000 population	763
Detected crimes	3,850

Road Traffic Collisions

Fatal RTCs	79
Total Injury RTCs	8,374

Health

Police days lost through sickness	40,407
Number of assaults on police	294

LOTHIAN AND BORDERS POLICE

Fettes Avenue, Edinburgh, EH4 1RB
Telephone 0131 311 3131
Website www.lbp.police.uk

Chief Constable; Sir Roy Cameron, Q.P.M. B.A. M.Phil.

Force General Statistics

Population of Force Area	884,900
Size of Force Area km²	6,595
Annual expenditure (£ million)	143.56
Cost per resident per day	44p

Force divisions and staff

Number of territorial divisions	6
Total number of officers	2,584
Total number of Specials	207
Total number of civilian support staff	1,063

Calls from the public

Number of emergency calls	N/k
Calls for service	N/k

Crime

Recorded crimes	84,106
Crimes per 10,000 population	950
Detected crimes	35,325

Road Traffic Collisions

Fatal RTCs	48
Total Injury RTCs	3,186

Health

Police days lost through sickness	30,624
Number of assaults on police	N/k

LEICESTERSHIRE CONSTABULARY

St. John's, Narborough, Leicester, LE9 5BX
Telephone 0116 222 2222
Website www.leics.police.uk

Chief Constable; Mr D.J. Wyrko, Q.P.M. B.Sc

Force General Statistics

Population of Force Area	928,700
Size of Force Area km²	2,553
Annual expenditure (£ million)	105.91
Cost per resident per day	31p

Force divisions and staff

Number of territorial divisions	5
Total number of officers	1,992
Total number of Specials	247
Total number of civilian support staff	872

Calls from the public

Number of emergency calls	147,905
Calls for service	359,148

Crime

Recorded crimes	94,577
Crimes per 10,000 population	1,018
Detected crimes	28,722

Road Traffic Collisions

Fatal RTCs	86
Total Injury RTCs	5,058

Health

Police days lost through sickness	25,079
Number of assaults on police	218

LINCOLNSHIRE POLICE

PO Box 999, Lincoln, LN5 7PH
Telephone 01522 532222
Website www.lincs.police.uk

Chief Constable; Mr R.J.N. Childs, Q.P.M. B.Sc.

Force General Statistics

Population of Force Area	625,744
Size of Force Area km²	5,918
Annual expenditure (£ million)	68.97
Cost per resident per day	30p

Force divisions and staff

Number of territorial divisions	3
Total number of officers	1,116
Total number of Specials	195
Total number of civilian support staff	537

Calls from the public

Number of emergency calls	66,665
Calls for service	144,386

Crime

Recorded crimes	46,170
Crimes per 10,000 population	738
Detected crimes	12,931

Road Traffic Collisions

Fatal RTCs	104
Total Injury RTCs	3,947

Health

Police days lost through sickness	13,519
Number of assaults on police	128

LONDON, METROPOLITAN POLICE SERVICE

New Scotland Yard, Broadway, London, SW1H 0BG
Telephone 020 7230 1212
Website www.met.police.uk

Commissioner; Sir John Stevens, Q.P.M. LL.B. M.Phil. C.I.Mgt

Force General Statistics

Population of Force Area	7,683,489
Size of Force Area km²	2,069
Annual expenditure (£ million)	1,834.62
Cost per resident per day	65p

Force divisions and staff

Number of territorial divisions	33 (Boroughs)
Total number of officers	25,464
Total number of Specials	703
Total number of civilian support staff	11,430

Calls from the public

Number of emergency calls	2,412,981
Calls for service	3,605,575

Crime

Recorded crimes	1,052,047
Crimes per 10,000 population	1,369
Detected crimes	166,196

Road Traffic Collisions

Fatal RTCs	290
Total Injury RTCs	48,226

Health

Police days lost through sickness	13,519
Number of assaults on police	128

MERSEYSIDE POLICE

PO Box 59, Liverpool, L69 1JD
Telephone 0151 709 6010
Website www.merseyside.police.uk

Chief Constable; Mr N. Bettison, Q.P.M. M.A. M.B.A.

Force General Statistics

Population of Force Area	1,409,371
Size of Force Area km²	648
Annual expenditure (£ million)	245.09
Cost per resident per day	48p

Force divisions and staff

Number of territorial divisions	4 (Districts)
Total number of officers	4,084
Total number of Specials	476
Total number of civilian support staff	476

Calls from the public

Number of emergency calls	292,549
Calls for service	587,788

Crime

Recorded crimes	148,172
Crimes per 10,000 population	1,051
Detected crimes	38,648

Road Traffic Collisions

Fatal RTCs	55
Total Injury RTCs	9,959

Health

Police days lost through sickness	49,678
Number of assaults on police	520

NORFOLK CONSTABULARY

Martineau Lane, Norwich, NR1 2 DJ
Telephone 01603 768769
Website www.norfolk.police.uk

Chief Constable; Mr K.R. Williams, Q.P.M. B.A.

Force General Statistics

Population of Force Area	795,600
Size of Force Area km²	5,385
Annual expenditure (£ million)	86.57
Cost per resident per day	30p

Force divisions and staff

Number of territorial divisions	3
Total number of officers	1,382
Total number of Specials	285
Total number of civilian support staff	692

Calls from the public

Number of emergency calls	82,340
Calls for service	175,407

Crime

Recorded crimes	59,387
Crimes per 10,000 population	746
Detected crimes	18,063

Road Traffic Collisions

Fatal RTCs	71
Total Injury RTCs	3,975

Health

Police days lost through sickness	17,497
Number of assaults on police	294

NORTHAMPTONSHIRE POLICE

Wootton Hall, Northampton, NN4 0JQ
Telephone 01604 700700
Website www.norpol.police.uk

Chief Constable; Mr C.Fox, Q.P.M. B.Sc. D.I.S.

Force General Statistics

Population of Force Area	615,796
Size of Force Area km^2	2,637
Annual expenditure (£ million)	66.87
Cost per resident per day	30p

Force divisions and staff

Number of territorial divisions	4
Total number of officers	1,117
Total number of Specials	199
Total number of civilian support staff	616

Calls from the public

Number of emergency calls	84,243
Calls for service	138,128

Crime

Recorded crimes	61,240
Crimes per 10,000 population	994
Detected crimes	19,945

Road Traffic Collisions

Fatal RTCs	76
Total Injury RTCs	3,346

Health

Police days lost through sickness	12,081
Number of assaults on police	189

NORTHERN CONSTABULARY

Old Perth Road, Inverness, IV1 3SY
Telephone 01463 715555
Website www.northern.police.uk

Chief Constable; Mr W.A. Robertson, Q.P.M. LL.B. M.Phil.

Force General Statistics

Population of Force Area	278,500
Size of Force Area km²	30,397
Annual expenditure (£ million)	41.42
Cost per resident per day	41p

Force divisions and staff

Number of territorial divisions	8
Total number of officers	653
Total number of Specials	413
Total number of civilian support staff	361

Calls from the public

Number of emergency calls	N/k
Calls for service	N/k

Crime

Recorded crimes	12,839
Crimes per 10,000 population	461
Detected crimes	7,190

Road Traffic Collisions

Fatal RTCs	35
Total Injury RTCs	909

Health

Police days lost through sickness	6,234
Number of assaults on police	N/k

NORTH YORKSHIRE POLICE

Newby Wiske Hall, Northallerton, North Yorkshire, DL7 9HA
Telephone 01609 783131
Website - No current website

Chief Constable; Mr D.R Kenworthy, Q.P.M.

Force General Statistics

Population of Force Area	737,600
Size of Force Area km²	8,312
Annual expenditure (£ million)	8,312
Cost per resident per day	28p

Force divisions and staff

Number of territorial divisions	3
Total number of officers	1,284
Total number of Specials	217
Total number of civilian support staff	512

Calls from the public

Number of emergency calls	75,513
Calls for service	224,169

Crime

Recorded crimes	53,554
Crimes per 10,000 population	726
Detected crimes	16,652

Road Traffic Collisions

Fatal RTCs	68
Total Injury RTCs	4,847

Health

Police days lost through sickness	16,944
Number of assaults on police	104

NOTTINGHAMSHIRE CONSTABULARY

Sherwood Lodge, Arnold, Nottingham
Telephone 0115 967 0999
Website www.nottinghamshire.police.uk

Chief Constable; Mr C.M. Green, M.A.

Force General Statistics

Population of Force Area	1,031,687
Size of Force Area km^2	2,209
Annual expenditure (£ million)	128.1
Cost per resident per day	34p

Force divisions and staff

Number of territorial divisions	5
Total number of officers	2,224
Total number of Specials	426
Total number of civilian support staff	1,046

Calls from the public

Number of emergency calls	199,583
Calls for service	372,415

Crime

Recorded crimes	136,875
Crimes per 10,000 population	1,327
Detected crimes	29,367

Road Traffic Collisions

Fatal RTCs	64
Total Injury RTCs	5,727

Health

Police days lost through sickness	31,457
Number of assaults on police	422

POLICE SERVICE OF NORTHERN IRELAND

'Brooklyn', Knock Road, Belfast, BT5 6LE
Telephone 028 90 650222
Website www.psni.police.uk

Acting Chief Constable; Colin Cramphorn

Force General Statistics

Population of Force Area	1,547,300
Size of Force Area km²	14,145
Annual expenditure (£ million)	654
Cost per resident per day	115

Force divisions and staff

Number of territorial divisions	12
Total number of officers	8,393
Total number of Specials	3,840
Total number of civilian support staff	N/k

Calls from the public

Number of emergency calls	110,960
Calls for service	N/k

Crime

Recorded crimes	119,111
Crimes per 10,000 population	770
Detected crimes	36,004

Road Traffic Collisions

Fatal RTCs	150
Total Injury RTCs	13,893

Health

Police days lost through sickness	N/k
Number of assaults on police	N/k

SOUTH WALES POLICE

Cowbridge Road, Bridgend, CF31 3SU
Telephone 01656 655555
Website www.south-wales.police.uk

Chief Constable; Mr A.T.Burden, Q.P.M. B.Sc.(Hons)

Force General Statistics

Population of Force Area	1,239,279
Size of Force Area km²	2,072
Annual expenditure (£ million)	165.63
Cost per resident per day	37p

Force divisions and staff

Number of territorial divisions	7
Total number of officers	2,961
Total number of Specials	269
Total number of civilian support staff	1,227

Calls from the public

Number of emergency calls	252,018
Calls for service	547,866

Crime

Recorded crimes	127,040
Crimes per 10,000 population	1025
Detected crimes	39,079

Road Traffic Collisions

Fatal RTCs	62
Total Injury RTCs	5,107

Health

Police days lost through sickness	N/k
Number of assaults on police	317

SOUTH YORKSHIRE POLICE

Snig Hill, Sheffield, S3 8LY
Telephone 0114 220 2020
Website www.southyorks.police.uk

Chief Constable; Mr I.I. Heges, Q.P.M. LL.B.

Force General Statistics

Population of Force Area	1,304,192
Size of Force Area km²	1,561
Annual expenditure (£ million)	171.32
Cost per resident per day	36p

Force divisions and staff

Number of territorial divisions	11
Total number of officers	3,152
Total number of Specials	205
Total number of civilian support staff	1,380

Calls from the public

Number of emergency calls	218,006
Calls for service	450,965

Crime

Recorded crimes	131,700
Crimes per 10,000 population	1010
Detected crimes	32,404

Road Traffic Collisions

Fatal RTCs	50
Total Injury RTCs	6,761

Health

Police days lost through sickness	41,611
Number of assaults on police	198

STAFFORDSHIRE POLICE

Cannock Road, Stafford, ST17 0QG
Telephone 01785 257717
Website www.staffordshire.police.uk

Chief Constable; Mr J.W. Giffard, Q.P.M. B.A.(Hons)

Force General Statistics

Population of Force Area	1,062,759
Size of Force Area km²	2,716
Annual expenditure (£ million)	127.65
Cost per resident per day	33p

Force divisions and staff

Number of territorial divisions	4
Total number of officers	2,169
Total number of Specials	482
Total number of civilian support staff	882

Calls from the public

Number of emergency calls	136,256
Calls for service	362,659

Crime

Recorded crimes	98,852
Crimes per 10,000 population	930
Detected crimes	22,221

Road Traffic Collisions

Fatal RTCs	55
Total Injury RTCs	6,253

Health

Police days lost through sickness	27,460
Number of assaults on police	429

STRATHCLYDE POLICE

173, Pitt Street, Glasgow, G2 4JS
Telephone 0141 532 2000
Website www.strathclyde.police.uk

Chief Constable; Mr J. Orr, O.B.E., Q.P.M., LLD., B.A., C.I.Mgt

Force General Statistics

Population of Force Area	2,268,600
Size of Force Area km²	13,851
Annual expenditure (£ million)	377.73
Cost per resident per day	46p

Force divisions and staff

Number of territorial divisions	9
Total number of officers	7,116
Total number of Specials	322
Total number of civilian support staff	2,052

Calls from the public

Number of emergency calls	N/k
Calls for service	N/k

Crime

Recorded crimes	205,467
Crimes per 10,000 population	906
Detected crimes	88,351

Road Traffic Collisions

Fatal RTCs	98
Total Injury RTCs	6,943

Health

Police days lost through sickness	N/k
Number of assaults on police	88,017

SUFFOLK CONSTABULARY

Martlesham Heath, Ipswich, IP5 7QS
Telephone 01473 613500
Website www.suffolk.police.uk

Chief Constable; Mr P.J. Scott-Lee, Q.P.M.

Force General Statistics

Population of Force Area	671,095
Size of Force Area km²	3,802
Annual expenditure (£ million)	69.6
Cost per resident per day	28p

Force divisions and staff

Number of territorial divisions	3
Total number of officers	1,145
Total number of Specials	391
Total number of civilian support staff	631

Calls from the public

Number of emergency calls	88,740
Calls for service	132,761

Crime

Recorded crimes	43,355
Crimes per 10,000 population	646
Detected crimes	15,570

Road Traffic Collisions

Fatal RTCs	48
Total Injury RTCs	3,096

Health

Police days lost through sickness	12,513
Number of assaults on police	129

SURREY POLICE

Mount browne, Sandy Lane, Guildford, GU3 1HG
Telephone 01483 571212
Website www.surrey.police.uk

Chief Constable; Mr D. O'Connor, Q.P.M.

Force General Statistics

Population of Force Area	786,730
Size of Force Area km²	1,468
Annual expenditure (£ million)	91.43
Cost per resident per day	32p

Force divisions and staff

Number of territorial divisions	7
Total number of officers	1,785
Total number of Specials	175
Total number of civilian support staff	779

Calls from the public

Number of emergency calls	102,628
Calls for service	165,467

Crime

Recorded crimes	42,467 (1999)
Crimes per 10,000 population	540 (1999)
Detected crimes	14,819

Road Traffic Collisions

Fatal RTCs	57
Total Injury RTCs	6,147

Health

Police days lost through sickness	19,753
Number of assaults on police	140

SUSSEX POLICE

Malling House,Lewes, BN7 2DZ
Telephone 0845 60 70 999
Website www.sussex.police.uk

Chief Constable (Acting); Mrs Maria Wallis, Q.P.M.

Force General Statistics

Population of Force Area	1,498,900
Size of Force Area km^2	3,785
Annual expenditure (£ million)	167.99
Cost per resident per day	31p

Force divisions and staff

Number of territorial divisions	9
Total number of officers	2,810
Total number of Specials	357
Total number of civilian support staff	1,426

Calls from the public

Number of emergency calls	201,365
Calls for service	375,253

Crime

Recorded crimes	136,566
Crimes per 10,000 population	911
Detected crimes	33,953

Road Traffic Collisions

Fatal RTCs	93
Total Injury RTCs	8,263

Health

Police days lost through sickness	32,473
Number of assaults on police	402

TAYSIDE POLICE

PO Box 59, West Bell Street, Dundee, DD1 9JU
Telephone 01382 223200
Website www.tayside.police.uk

Chief Constable; Mr W.A Spence, Q.P.M. LL.B. B.A.

Force General Statistics

Population of Force Area	388,300
Size of Force Area km²	7,501
Annual expenditure (£ million)	60.82
Cost per resident per day	43p

Force divisions and staff

Number of territorial divisions	3
Total number of officers	1,138
Total number of Specials	156
Total number of civilian support staff	476

Calls from the public

Number of emergency calls	N/k
Calls for service	N/k

Crime

Recorded crimes	31,737
Crimes per 10,000 population	817
Detected crimes	13,012

Road Traffic Collisions

Fatal RTCs	34
Total Injury RTCs	1,254

Health

Police days lost through sickness	16,246
Number of assaults on police	N/k

THAMES VALLEY POLICE

Kidlington, Oxon, OX5 2NX
Telephone 01865 846000
Website www.thamesvalley.police.uk

Chief Constable; Mr P. Neyroud

Force General Statistics

Population of Force Area	2,086,811
Size of Force Area km²	5,749
Annual expenditure (£ million)	222.42
Cost per resident per day	29p

Force divisions and staff

Number of territorial divisions	10
Total number of officers	3,740
Total number of Specials	472
Total number of civilian support staff	1,844

Calls from the public

Number of emergency calls	285,747
Calls for service	518,124

Crime

Recorded crimes	191,875
Crimes per 10,000 population	919
Detected crimes	38,735

Road Traffic Collisions

Fatal RTCs	150
Total Injury RTCs	11,865

Health

Police days lost through sickness	53,509
Number of assaults on police	142

WARWICKSHIRE CONSTABULARY

PO Box 4, Leek Wootton, Warwick, CV35 7QB
Telephone 01926 415000
Website www.warwickshire.police.uk

Chief Constable; Mr A.C. Timpson, B.A. (Econ)(Hons)

Force General Statistics

Population of Force Area	506,701
Size of Force Area km²	1,979
Annual expenditure (£ million)	54.83
Cost per resident per day	30p

Force divisions and staff

Number of territorial divisions	2
Total number of officers	899
Total number of Specials	260
Total number of civilian support staff	395

Calls from the public

Number of emergency calls	67,219
Calls for service	153,607

Crime

Recorded crimes	38,593
Crimes per 10,000 population	762
Detected crimes	8,667

Road Traffic Collisions

Fatal RTCs	50
Total Injury RTCs	3,217

Health

Police days lost through sickness	13,090
Number of assaults on police	142

WEST MERCIA CONSTABULARY

Hindlip Hall, Hindlip, PO Box 55, Worcester WR3 8SP
Telephone 01905 723000
Website www.westmercia.police.uk

Chief Constable; Mr P. Hampson, Q.P.M. LL.B. A.K.C.

Force General Statistics

Population of Force Area	1,136,332
Size of Force Area km²	7,429
Annual expenditure (£ million)	116.21
Cost per resident per day	28p

Force divisions and staff

Number of territorial divisions	6
Total number of officers	1,890
Total number of Specials	476
Total number of civilian support staff	1,058

Calls from the public

Number of emergency calls	144,960
Calls for service	399,751

Crime

Recorded crimes	84,797
Crimes per 10,000 population	746
Detected crimes	24,307

Road Traffic Collisions

Fatal RTCs	75
Total Injury RTCs	6,008

Health

Police days lost through sickness	27,141
Number of assaults on police	373

WEST MIDLANDS POLICE

PO Box 52, Lloyd House, Colmore Circus Queensway, Birmingham, B4 6NQ
Telephone 0121 626 5000
Website www.west-midlands.police.uk

Chief Constable; Mr E. Crew, Q.P.M. O.St.J. D.L.

Force General Statistics

Population of Force Area	2,628,200
Size of Force Area km^2	899
Annual expenditure (£ million)	372.47
Cost per resident per day	39p

Force divisions and staff

Number of territorial divisions	21
Total number of officers	7,214
Total number of Specials	680
Total number of civilian support staff	2,880

Calls from the public

Number of emergency calls	561,511
Calls for service	897,850

Crime

Recorded crimes	364,887
Crimes per 10,000 population	1,388
Detected crimes	99,286

Road Traffic Collisions

Fatal RTCs	89
Total Injury RTCs	13,559

Health

Police days lost through sickness	90,046
Number of assaults on police	941

WEST YORKSHIRE POLICE

PO Box 9, Wakefield, West Yorkshire, WF1 3QP
Telephone 01924 375222
Website www.westyorkshire.police.uk

Chief Constable; Mr G. Moore, Q.P.M. B.A.(Hons)

Force General Statistics

Population of Force Area	2,113,300
Size of Force Area km²	2,015
Annual expenditure (£ million)	283.56
Cost per resident per day	37p

Force divisions and staff

Number of territorial divisions	17
Total number of officers	4,822
Total number of Specials	484
Total number of civilian support staff	2,315

Calls from the public

Number of emergency calls	432,838
Calls for service	3697,235

Crime

Recorded crimes	260,237
Crimes per 10,000 population	1,231
Detected crimes	65,245

Road Traffic Collisions

Fatal RTCs	111
Total Injury RTCs	13,641

Health

Police days lost through sickness	55,255
Number of assaults on police	665

WILTSHIRE CONSTABULARY

London Road, Devizes, Wiltshire, SN10 2DN
Telephone 01380 722341
Website www.wiltshire.police.uk

Chief Constable; Miss E. Neville, Q.P.M. M.A. Ph.D.

Force General Statistics

Population of Force Area	605,5050
Size of Force Area km^2	3,475
Annual expenditure (£ million)	69.06
Cost per resident per day	31p

Force divisions and staff

Number of territorial divisions	3
Total number of officers	1,119
Total number of Specials	173
Total number of civilian support staff	478

Calls from the public

Number of emergency calls	53,801
Calls for service	188,630

Crime

Recorded crimes	38,461
Crimes per 10,000 population	635
Detected crimes	12,815

Road Traffic Collisions

Fatal RTCs	49
Total Injury RTCs	3,426

Health

Police days lost through sickness	10,827
Number of assaults on police	108

CHAPTER 9. OTHER POLICE FORCES

1. Belfast Harbour Police
Port Operations Centre, Milewater Basin, Dufferin Road, Belfast. BT3 9AF
Tel (01232) 553000

2. Belfast International Airport Constabulary
Belfast International Airport, Belfast. BT29 4AB
Tel (01849) 42288

3. British Transport Police
PO Box 260, 15 Tavistock Place, London. WC1H 9SJ
Tel (0171) 388 7541

4. Falmouth Docks & Engineering Co. Ltd
The Docks, Falmouth, Cornwall. TR11 4NR
Tel (01326) 212100

5. Great Yarmouth Port Authority
20-21 South Quay, Great Yarmouth, Norfolk. NR30 2RE
Tel (01493) 335500

6. Isle of Man Aviation Security
Isle of Man Airport, Ballasalla, Isle of Man. IM9 2AS
Tel (01624 821603)

7. Isle of Man Port Services
Sea Terminal Building, Douglas, Isle of Man. IM1 2RF
Tel (01624) 686630

8. Larne Harbour Police
Larne Harbour Limited, Older Fleet Road, Larne Harbour, County Antrim. BT40 1AS
Tel (028) 2827 9223

9. London Port of Tilbury Police
Eastern Road, Tilbury Freeport, Tilbury, Essex. RM18 7DU
Tel (01375) 846781

10. Mersey Tunnels Police
Merseyside Passenger Transport Authority, The Mersey Tunnels, Georges Dock Building,
Pier Head, Liverpool. L3 1DD
Tel (0151) 236 8602

11. Ministry of Defence Police
Wethersfield, Braintree, Essex. CM7 4AZ
Tel (01371) 854000

12. National Crime Squad
PO Box 2500, London. SW1V 2WF
Tel (020) 7238 2500

13. National Criminal Intelligence Service
PO Box 8000, London. SE11 5EN
Tel (020) 7238 8000

14. Port of Bristol Police
Royal Portbury Dock, Bristol. BS20 9XQ
Tel (0117) 9820000

15. Port of Dover Police
Police Station, Eastern Docks, Dover. CT16 1JA
Tel (01304) 216084

16. Port of Flexitowe Police
Police Department, Felixtowe Dock and Railway Company, The Dock, Felixtowe,
Suffolk. IP11 8SY
Tel (01394) 604747

17. Port of Liverpool Police
Headquarters Liverpool Freeport, Liverpool. L21 1JD
Tel (0151) 949 1212

18. Royal Air Force Police
HQ Provost and Security Services, RAF Henlow, Bedfordshire. SG16 6DN
Tel (01462) 851515

19. Royal Botanic Gardens Constabulary
Kew, Richmond, Surrey. TW9 3AB
Tel (020) 8332 5121

20. Royal Marines Police
Headquarters Royal Marines, West Battery, Whale Island, Portsmouth, Hants. PO2 8DX
Tel (023) 9254 7548

21. Royal Military Police
Roussillon Barracks, Chichester, West Sussex. PO19 4BN
Tel (01243) 534342

22. Royal Naval Regulating Branch
Room 202, Victory Building, HM Naval Base, Portsmouth. PO1 3LS
Tel (023) 9272 7243

23. Royal Parks Constabulary
The Old Police House, Hyde Park, London. W2 2UH
Tel (020) 7298 2000

24. Tees & Hartlepool Port Authority Ltd
Harbour Police, Harbourmaster's Office, Tees Dock, Grangetown, Middlesborough,
Cleveland. TS6 6UD
Tel (01642) 277215

25. United Kingdom Atomic Energy Authority Constabulary
Building E6, Culham Science Centre, Abingdon, Oxfordshire. OX14 3DB
Tel (01235) 464105

CHAPTER 10. POLICE VEHICLES

The police have used cars and other types of vehicle almost since they were invented, but it was not until the 1960s and the inception of the panda car that they have become so familiar.

In recent times, it is safe to say that almost every mass manufacturer of vehicles has supplied or does supply vehicles to the police.

There are certain cars that will hold significant places in police vehicle history. The Jaguar Mk2, Morris Minor, Rover's P6 and SD1 V8, and perhaps the longest serving of all, the Range Rover. Its power and speed with its ability to pull an articulated lorry made it the first choice for motorway use. Sadly it seems that the Range Rover as a marked patrol car will soon be no more, it is now very much a luxury car at the top end of Land Rover's range. Pretenders to its throne come from Mercedes' ML series, and most of Japans four-by-four ranges.

Cars

There are several areas of use for cars in the police service, and each force will use models for each purpose according to their own criteria of cost, performance, or perhaps local links with the manufacturer.

General patrol or 'panda cars' are usually two or four door small to medium saloon or hatchback models. They must be economical, with little requirement for performance. Selected models will be mass-produced, so that parts and servicing are cheap and easily available. Most are now diesel-engined for economy. Popular at the moment are the Vauxhall Astra, Ford Focus and Rover 200, though smaller cars such as the Rover 100, Ford Fiesta, or Vauxhall Corsa are common, particularly in the city centre areas.

Intermediate cars are used for many purposes; in general policing terms they will be the 'response' cars, requiring a higher level of performance in order to respond to immediate incidents. In most forces a higher level of training is required for officers in this role. Current models in this role are cars such as the Ford Mondeo, Vauxhall Vectra, Nissan Primera and Peugeot's 406, with engines in the petrol range of 1.8 to 2 litres.

For roles such as traffic, motorway patrol, armed response or V.I.P. escort duties, where higher speeds and the requirement to carry a lot of equipment or more than two officers may be anticipated, then the big cars of a manufacturers range are considered. Current favourite is Volvo's S70/V70 T-5. This car has a good load carrying capability, has a host of safety features and is of course fast. BMW 3 and 5 series cars are also popular, as is Vauxhall's Omega V6. However, as in all other roles, the 'traditional' marques cannot always rely on a place in the police garage. Jaguar (X-type), Isuzu, Nissan, Volkswagen and many others, all now feature.

Officers driving these cars will be trained to advanced level, and for some roles, specific training in subjects such as defensive/evasive tactics may be given.

Volvo's S70/V70 T-5

Forces may have identified the need for particular cars for local needs and some quite interesting cars have been used. Greater Manchester Police deployed unmarked Ford Sierra RS Cosworths to fight vehicle crime with their X Cars department. Other forces are using and evaluating the phenomenal rally bred Subaru Impreza Prodrive or Mitsubishi Evolution 6. This type of vehicle, unlike many of the big cars used by the police, is fitted with few luxury items but has tremendous handling and performance. In the hands of a highly trained police driver, there really is no getting away from one. In the areas where these cars are used there have been significant reductions in car crime.

In some forces there are specific requirements that call for the expense of luxury cars that may be armoured for the transport of VIPs, where this is a regular requirement.
Most forces have an armoured vehicle such as a Land Rover or Range Rover for use in firearms incidents.

Motorcycles

The police use of motorcycles is mostly for traffic patrolling, though some may be used for surveillance operations where their ability to cut through traffic unobtrusively is invaluable. The requirement is for a motorcycle that is powerful enough to carry rider, radio and patrol equipment. It must be quick and handle well in all conditions, but must be comfortable to ride for long periods of time. It must also be able to trundle along for hours at walking

The Honda ST 1100 Pan European

speed, for the escort of abnormal loads, ceremonial parades or demonstrations.

Since the demise of the British motorcycle industry as it was in the 1970s, the police have almost exclusively used BMW bikes. The various touring models all being popular. More recently, the Honda ST1100 Pan European has proved to be effective.

Again there are niches for other types and many forces have bought small trail bikes for town centres, where they are less cumbersome than the big tourers. For 'unmarked' roles, as with cars, almost any make or model of bike can be utilised.

Vans

Originally, the police 'black mariah' was the vehicle in which prisoners were taken away. Vans now are mostly used for policing public order, able to carry and easily deploy numbers of officers, in full riot gear if needed. They are invariably now fitted with a secure cage for the transport of potentially violent prisoners. The load carrying strength of a commercial vehicle chassis also means that protective armour or mesh can be fitted, together with sophisticated fire extinguishers and recirculatory air-conditioning. Ford's Transit mostly dominates this role, although Mercedes and Volkswagen are producing models that are being bought in increasing numbers.

For the carrying of dogs, most forces use 'car-derived vans' with vehicles such as the Vauxhall Astra van being the popular type. These will be fitted with cages in the back for the dogs and also ventilation systems to keep the animals comfortable, as they may have to remain in the vehicle for long periods.

Other vehicles

The police have found a need for almost every kind of vehicle. Lorries and vans with specially built bodies are used for underwater search units, scientific support teams, firearms units and as command centres or mobile incident rooms.

Manufacturers are always keen to see the police use their vehicles. It is an instant and high profile endorsement of the product. It will probably be the most demanding role that a vehicle could be put to, many of the patrol vehicles virtually never get cold, and they are run twenty-four hours a day. As such it pays the manufacturer to sell the cars to the police at the most rock bottom prices. Purchase price is always a factor in choosing a vehicle for a job.

For publicity, manufacturers of vehicles or vehicle equipment have dressed up certain models that the police will be unlikely to ever buy. There have been Lotus Esprit Turbo cars and a Honda CBR900 Fireblade in full police livery. Grampian Police even had a Jaguar XJ220 marked up!

Over the years individual forces have developed their own liveries for their marked cars. These reflect the importance of being easily seen, particularly in poor conditions, and also

Armoured RUC Land Rover.

to show a corporate image for the force. Recent research has now come up with the best markings for high visibility, and it is likely that all forces will soon be adopting the same markings and colours. The preferred pattern appears to be blocks of yellow and blue, highly reflective material. The rear of the vehicle will be red and yellow, with just the red being reflective, to comply with construction and use regulations.

There is no doubt that police vehicles will have to become more sophisticated and further modified from the original car. Vehicles of the near future must comply with health and safety regulations, and consider human rights. The need to deploy ever more electronic equipment such as radios, mobile telephones and in the near future, computer terminals, will figure in vehicle design and choice. More will be fitted with compartments for arrested persons, and air conditioning and the most up to date safety features will be within the specifications.

CHAPTER 11. AVIATION

The use of aircraft by the Police in the United Kingdom and indeed across the world, has grown hugely in recent years. Aircraft, both rotary winged (helicopters) and fixed winged (aeroplanes) are now used by all forces in Britain.

They provide for airborne observation of incidents and have proved invaluable in pursuits, allowing patrols on the ground to stay back from cars being pursued, thereby making the situation safer. Aircraft also provide co-ordination for major incidents such as multiple road traffic collisions, by being able to fly over them and get a birds' eye view of what is going on and being able to either co-ordinate operations directly or to provide live TV down links to a commander on the ground below or even back at a police station or other site. Not every force has it's own aircraft however, as they are very expensive to buy and operate. Many of the smaller forces have joined together to form consortia to share an aircraft, and some other forces share an aircraft with ambulance services. Neighbouring forces also often have agreed policies of calling on the services of each other's aircraft, should the need arise. This is useful where, in the absence of a consortium, one force with a helicopter has need of a fixed wing aircraft.

It has proven to be cost effective to lease machines, and most of the countries police aircraft are leased from companies such as McAlpine. This way it is cheaper to maintain the modernity of the aircraft, and if one needs to go for servicing, then the leasing company can provide a replacement.

Crew

The pilots of UK police aircraft are civilian pilots, who will usually have a military background. The military use of helicopters and light aircraft parallels in many ways with the way that police aircraft are deployed. These pilots are generally employed not by the police force, but by the leasing company.

The observers and other crew will be police officers. The commander of the aircraft will be a police sergeant or above, he will be the officer who directs where the aircraft goes and what it does, although the pilot has ultimate responsibility for it and will keep it within it's operational 'envelope' and within what is permitted by CAA rules and air traffic control.

The other police crew will operate cameras, lights and radios to police on the ground.

For those aircraft where the ambulance service has joint use, the police crew may be ditched and ambulance paramedics and a doctor will take their places. Or there may be a requirement for a mixed crew for a particular deployment. This will be dependant on the size of the aircraft.

The Aircraft

Most police aircraft are helicopters for the simple reason that they can take off and land vertically without the need for an airstrip and of course they can hover and change direction sharply. Fixed wing aircraft on the other hand usually have broader weather capabilities, can spend much longer in the air and are faster (There are increasing numbers of high performance cars that can outrun, in speed and endurance, most helicopters in a straight line, such as a motorway).

Aircraft are a platform for an ever-increasing array of equipment. This may include:
Stills cameras
Video cameras
Video camera with microwave down-link (this can beam live pictures to a command point or even cars on the ground)
Infra-red cameras
Gyro-stabilized forward-looking infra-red (FLIR) camera
Image intensifying cameras
Binoculars

GPS systems
Radios for air traffic, police and/or other emergency service channels
Mobile telephone link.

High powered spot or floodlights (such as 'Nitesun')
Loud hailer system ('Skyshout')

Those aircraft also used for emergency medical services will also carry sophisticated pre-hospital emergency care equipment and stretchers.

Forces whose aircraft are likely to be deployed over water, will also fit emergency liferafts.

Air Support Unit	Aircraft
Cambridge	Eurocopter AS 355 Squirrel
Central Counties	Eurocopter EC135T
Cheshire	BN2B-20 Islander
Chilterns	Eurocopter EC135T
Devon & Cornwall	Eurocopter/Kawasaki BK 117
Dorset	MD902 Explorer
Dyfed-Powys	Augusta 109E
East Midlands	Eurocopter EC135T
Essex	AS 355 Squirrel
Greater Manchester Police	Eurocopter AS 355 Squirrel
Hampshire	BN2B-20 Islander
Humberside	Bolkow BK105
Lancashire	Eurocopter AS 355 Squirrel
Merseyside	Eurocopter AS 355 Squirrel
Norfolk	Bolkow 105DB
North East Police	Eurocopter EC135T BN2B-20 300 Islander BN2B-20 300 Islander
North Midlands	Eurocopter AS 355 Squirrel
North Wales Police	Eurocopter EC135T
Northamptonshire Police	Eurocopter EC135T
Royal Ulster Constabulary G.C.	BN2T Islander
South & East Wales	Eurocopter AS 355 Squirrel Bolkow BO105DB
Metropolitan Police Service & Surrey	Eurocopter AS 355 Squirrel
South Yorkshire	Eurocopter AS 355 Squirrel
Sussex	MD902 Explorer
Western Counties	AS355F2
West Midlands	MD902 Explorer
West Yorkshire	Bolkow MBB105DBS4
Wiltshire	MD902 Explorer

Specifications

EUROCOPTER AS 355 SQUIRREL

Fuselage width	1.87 m
Weight empty	1,436 kg
Hovering ceiling	2,000 m
Maximum level speed	224 km/h
Maximum range	720 km
Service ceiling	3,800 m

EUROCOPTER EC 135

Fuselage width	2.65 m
Weight empty	1,490 kg
Hovering ceiling	1,325 m
Maximum level speed	138 knots
Maximum range	335 nm
Service ceiling	3,050 m

EUROCOPTER/KAWASAKI BK 117

Fuselage width	1.60 m
Weight empty	1,745 kg
Hovering ceiling	3,690 m
Maximum level speed	250 km/h
Maximum range	540 km
Service ceiling	5,480 m

EXPLORER MD902

Fuselage width	1.63 m
Weight empty	1,531 kg
Hovering ceiling	3,353 m
Maximum level speed	248 km/h
Maximum range	542 km
Service ceiling	5,335 m

AGUSTA A 109

Fuselage width	2.45 m
Weight empty	1,660 kg
Hovering ceiling	5,305 m
Maximum level speed	264 km/h
Maximum range	805 km
Service ceiling	6,100 m

BRITTEN-NORMAN 2B ISLANDER

Fuselage width	1.21 m
Weight empty	1,866 kg
Maximum level speed	274 km/h
Maximum range	931 km
Service ceiling	3,445 m

EUROCOPTER BO 105

Fuselage width	1.58 m
Weight empty	1,301 kg
Hovering ceiling	3,200 m
Maximum level speed	245 km/h
Maximum range	574 km
Service ceiling	1,700 m

Cheshire Constabulory, BNZB-20 Islander.

West Yorkshire Police, Bolklow MBB105DB54.

Dorset Police Explorer MD 902.

North Wales Police, Eurocopter EC135T.

Essex Police, AS355 Squirrel.

Essex Police, Eurocopter AS 355 Squirrel.

Merseyside Police, Eurocopter AS 355 Squirrel.

CHAPTER 12. PAY SCALES

Constables' pay

Completed years of service in rank

	Annual salaries as at 1st September 2001
On commencing service	17,733
On completion of initial training period	19,842
2	21,015
3	21,570
4	22,323
5	23,037
6	23,787
7	24,477
8	25,095
9	25,095
10	25,911
11	25,911
12	26,862
13	26,862
14	28,062
Single performance payments	28,881
	29,697

Sergeants' pay

Completed years of service in rank

0	27,084
1	28,062
2	29,040
3	30,027
4	30,675
5	31,590
Single performance payments	32,505
	33,423

Inspectors' & Chief Inspectors' pay

Completed years of service in rank
London salaries in brackets

0	35,034 (36,636)
1	36,066 (37,665)
2	37,095 (38,694)
3	38,124 (39,729)
4	39,153 (40,761)
5	39,960 (41,571)
6	40,773 (42,378)
Single performance payments	41,583 (43,185)
	42,309 (43,911)

Superintendents' pay

RANGE 1		RANGE 2	
Pay Point	Salary p.a.	Pay Point	Salary p.a.
1.	47,649	6.	55,581
2.	49,140	7.	56,547
3.	50,637	8.	57,786
4.	52,131	9.	59,151
5.	53,790		
6.	55,581		

Senior Police Officers

(Salary is often dependant on whether their appointment is for a fixed term or not)

Assistant Chief Constables	68,760 - 78,930
Designated Deputy Chief Constables	78,930 - or 80% of Chief Constable's salary whichever is higher

Chief Constables by population band:

1. Up to 500,000	82,407 - 94,245
2. 500,001 - 1,000,000	86,622 - 101,865
3. 1,000,001 - 2,000,000	94,245 - 109,482
4. More than 2,000,000	104,295 - 117,699

Chief Constables of Greater Manchester, Strathclyde & West Midlands	108,066 -121,962
RUC Chief Constables	122,556 - 131,718
Metropolitan Police Commander	68,760 - 78,930
Assistant Commissioner	109,482 - 122,556
Deputy Commissioner	128,793 - 138,423
City of London Commissioner	94,245 - 109,482
City of London Assistant Commissioner	78,930 or 80% of Commissioner's salary whichever is higher

CHAPTER 13. ABBREVIATIONS

ABH Actual Bodily Harm

ACC Assistant Chief Constable

ACPO Association of Chief Police Officers for England, Wales and Northern Ireland

ACPOS Association of Chief Police Officer for Scotland

AEAC Atomic Energy Authority Constabulary

AFO Authorised Firearms Officer

AFR Automatic Fingerprint Recognition

AI Accident Investigation/Investigator

ANPR Automatic Number Plate Recognition

APA Association of Police Authorities

APS Acting Police Sergeant

ARV Armed Response Vehicle

ARU Armed Response Unit

ASBO Anti-Social Behaviour Order

ASR Annual Strategic Review

ASU Air Support Unit

ASW Approved Social Worker

BAWP British Association of Women Police

BCU Basic Command Unit

BIAD Burglary In A Dwelling

BID Brought In Dead

BOTIAD Burglary Other Than In A Dwelling

BPA Black Police Association

BVPI Best Value Performance Indicator

C&D Complaints and Discipline Department

CAA Civil Aviation Authority

CAB Criminal Assets Bureau

CAD Computer Aided Despatch

CC Chief Constable

CC Crime Concern

CDC Central Detention Centre

CDRP Crime and Disorder Reduction Partnership

CFF Crime Fighting Fund

CHIS Covert Human Intelligence Source

CICA Criminal Injuries Compensation Agency

CICB Criminal Injuries Compensation Board (outdated term for CICA)

CID Criminal Investigation Department

CIO Chief Immigration Officer

CIS Criminal Intelligence System

CJAD Criminal Justice Administration Department

CJU Criminal Justice Unit

CMF Capital Modernisation Fund

CO Commissioner's Office

CPO Close Protection Officer

CPO Crime Prevention Officer

CPS Crown Prosecution Service

CPT Child Protection Team

CPT Community Police Team

CRO Criminal Records Office

CROP Covert Rural Observation Post

CRP Crime Reduction Partnership

CRR Community and Race Relations

CSB Crime Statistics Bulletin

CSO Community Safety Officer

CSO Community Service Order

CTO Central Ticket Office

CTR Close Target Reconnaissance

D&D Drunk and Disorderly

D&I Drunk and Incapable

DC Detective Constable

DCC Deputy Chief Constable

DCI Detective Chief Inspector

DI Detective Inspector

DLO Drug Liaison Officer

DOA Dead On Arrival

DPG Diplomatic Protection Group

DPO Data Protection Office/Officer

DPP Director of Public Prosecutions

DS Detective Sergeant

DTTU Defensive Tactics Training Unit

DVLA Driver and Vehicle Licensing Agency

DVO Domestic Violence Office/Officer

ECHR European Convention on Human Rights

EO Equal Opportunities

EOD Explosive Ordnance Disposal

EPO Emergency Protection Order

ET Employment Tribunal

FIB Force Investigation Bureau

FIO Field Intelligence Officer

FME Forensic Medical Examiner

FPN Fixed Penalty Notice

FSS Forensic Science Service

FSU Firearm Support Unit

FTC Force Training Centre

FTR Failed to Report

FTS Failed to Stop

GBFI Garda Bureau of Fraud Investigation

GBH Grievous Bodily Harm

GNDU Garda National Drugs Unit

GNTB Garda National Traffic Bureau

GP General Purpose

GRA Generic Risk Assessment

HBO Home Beat Officer

HMC&E Her Majesty's Customs and Excise

HOLMES Home Office Large and Major Enquiry System

HOSAF Home Office Special Aviation Fund

HR Human Resources

HRA Human Rights Act

IED Improvised Explosive Device

INDIS Immigration and Nationality Directorate Intelligence System

IPA International Police Association

IRV Immediate Response Vehicle

ISD Information Systems Department

LGPA Lesbian and Gay Police Association

LIO Local Intelligence Officer

LMS Local Monitoring System

LPU Local Policing Unit

MCU Major Crime Unit

MFH Missing From Home

MISPER Missing Person

MO Modus Operandi

MPS Metropolitan Police Service

NACRO National Association for the Care and Resettlement of Offenders

NBCI National Bureau of Criminal Investigation

NBPA National Black Police Association

NCIS National Criminal Intelligence Service

NCS National Crime Squads

NFA No Further Action

NFS National Forgery Section

NID National Informant Database

NIHC National Informant Handlers' Course

NIP Notice of Intended Prosecution

NIS National Identification Service

NIS National Investigation Service (Customs)

NMPH National Missing Persons Helpline

NOK Next Of Kin

NPF National Police Fund

NPT National Police Training

NRC National Reporting Centre

NSMU National Source Management Unit

NSY New Scotland Yard

OIC Officer in Charge

OP Observation Post

OSG Operational Support Group

OSU Operational Support Unit

OVTS Organised Vehicle Theft Section

PAA Police Authority Associations

PAD Police Advisory Board

PC Police Constable

PCA (Independent) Police Complaints Authority

PCCG Police Community Consultative Group

PDP Probationer Development Program

PDR Performance and Development Review

PF Police Federation of England and Wales

PFNI Police Federation of Northern Ireland

PFS Police Federation of Scotland

PIR Police Initial Recruitment

PITO Police Information Technology Organisation

PMAS Police Mutual Assurance Society

PMC Personnel Management Committee

PMU Personnel Management Unit

PNC Police National Computer

PNCB Police National Computer Bureau

PNLD Police National Legal Database

PNN Police National Network

POP Problem Oriented Policing

PPO Police Protection Order

PPP Police Performance Procedures

PR Personal Radio

PRAS Police Research Award Scheme

PRCU Policing and Reducing Crime Unit

PS Police Sergeant

PS Police Station

PS Police Surgeon

PSDB Police Scientific Development Branch

PSRCP Public Safety Radio Communications Project

PSRCS Public Safety Radio Communication System

PSU Police Support Unit

PSU Professional Standards Unit

PTC Police Training Centre

PTI Physical Training Instructor

PYO Persistent Young Offender

QPM Queen's Police Medal

RFTU Road Fuel Testing Unit

RI Rapid Intervention

RMTU Regional Management Training Unit

RTA Road Traffic Accident (outdated term for RTC)

RTC Road Traffic Collision

SB Special Branch

SC Special Constable/Constabulary

SDU Special Detective Unit

SEUPAT Social Exclusion Unit Policy Action Team

SFO Serious Fraud Office

SFO Specialist Firearms Officer

SIO Senior Investigating Officer

SIS Special Intelligence Section

SIT Special Initiative Team

SLA Service Level Agreement

SM Strategic Management

SOCO Scenes of Crime Officer

SPB Special Projects Branch

SPG Special Patrol Group

SSIB Strategic and Specialist Intelligence Branch

SSU Scientific Support Unit

SWAT Special Weapons And Tactics

TADA Taking and Driving Away

TAG Territorial Aid Group

TDO Trainer Development Officer

TGP Total Geographic Policing

TIC Taken Into Consideration

TPO Traffic Patrol Officer

TSG Territorial Support Group

TSU Technical Support Unit

TW Traffic Warden

TWOC Taking Without Owner's Consent

UBO Unit Beat Officer

UC Undercover Detective

UDT Unarmed Defensive Tactics

USU Underwater Search Unit

UTMV Unlawful Taking of Motor Vehicle

VEL Vehicle Excise Licence

VS Victim Support

VSS Victim Support Scheme

WLO Wildlife Liaison Officer

WPC Woman Police Constable (outdated term)

WPS Woman Police Sergeant (outdated term)

YJ Youth Justice

YOI Young Offender Institutions

YOT Youth Offending Team

ABOUT THE AUTHORS

1. Mike McBride

Mike McBride is a Bachelor of Science and the author of three books on operational policing, namely Street Survival Skills, Crime Patrol and the European Police Firearms. He has been a regular contributor to International Police Review on firearms topics and Prohibited and Concealable Weapons Review on officer safety. His consuming interest in policing has led to him editing Jane's Information Group Police and Security Equipment Yearbook. He has also chaired conferences, such as Jane's Managing Police Firearms Units, which was held in Maastrict and sponsored by National Police Training.

Although his writing consumes much of his spare time Mike is proud to be, first and foremost, a full-time police officer. In 1984 he joined the British police and was promoted to the rank of Inspector five years ago. He is currently serving in an operational role.

Mike is a member of the American Society for Law Enforcement Trainers and has delivered training to officers in North America.

E-mail   -   mike.mcbride@interramp.co.uk

Mike McBride.

2. Glyn Collins

Glyn Collins is a former Royal Marines Commando who joined the Police Service in 1987. He has been a firearms instructor since 1994, with particular interest and expertise in tactical first aid. He has taken part in a Police Research Group on 'Emergency Medical Care at Firearms Incidents', and developed the Police Tactical Emergency Care course, used by firearms and PSU medics in his force.

He is member of his force' sailing club, being an RYA skipper. He is also keen on motorcycling and music.

Glyn is at the rank of sergeant and is currently serving in an operational role.

This is his first involvement in a book.

E- mail   -   glyn.collins@rya-online.net

The views of the authors are not to be construed as representing police policy.

Glyn Collins.

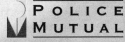

THE BRITISH
ARMY
a pocket guide
2002-2003

Charles Heyman

THE BRITISH
ARMY
a pocket guide
2002-2003
Charles Heyman

Since its inception in 1984, *The British Army - a pocket guide* has established itself as the market leader in this particular sphere of defence publishing.

This the eighth edition is completely up to date reflecting the current situation of the British Army and all of the changes being made. The book includes a new chapter focusing on the proposed Rapid Intervention Forces.

This guide is the only reference work to be recognised by the British Army Public Relations.

ISBN 085052 867 4
192 pages
Illustrated throughout
£4.95 Paperback

THE
ARMED FORCES
OF THE
UNITED KINGDOM
2001-2002

CHARLES HEYMAN

The Armed Forces of the United Kingdom 2001-2002
covers all the vital aspects of the organisations and
equipment of the UK Army, Royal Navy and the
Royal Air Force.

Silhouette outlines for major equipment and wiring
diagrams showing the details of all national military
organisations including an RN frigate, RAF squadron
and an Army infantry battalion.

It is essential reading for all those who wish to be
informed of the current state of the UK's defence force.

ISBN: 0 85052 804 6
192 pages
Illustrated throughout
£5.95 paperback

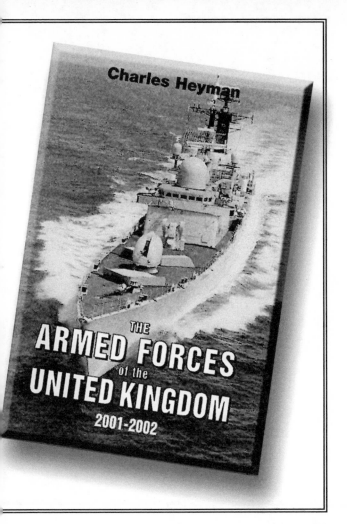

Charles Heyman

THE ARMED FORCES of the UNITED KINGDOM
2001-2002